THE DAWN'S EARLY LIGHT

THE DAWN'S EARLY LIGHT

by

JOSEPH M. STOWELL

MOODY PRESS
CHICAGO

© 1990 by
MOODY PRESS
JOSEPH M. STOWELL

All Scripture quotations, unless noted otherwise, are from the *New American Standard Bible*, © 1960, 1962, 1963, 1968, 1971, 1972, 1973, 1975, and 1977 by The Lockman Foundation, and are used by permission.

ISBN: 0-8024-7171-4

2 3 4 5 6 7 8 Printing/AF/Year 95 94 93 92 91 90

Printed in the United States of America

*This book is lovingly dedicated
to our children:
Joe, Libby, and Matt,
who will carry the torch of truth
into their generation if our Lord tarries.
May they have the courage and persistence
to embrace a clear commitment to truth
that the light of their lives may penetrate
the deepening darkness of their day
for the glory of Christ.*

Contents

PREFACE

America has dramatically changed.

In a swift forty years we have shifted from the values that made our nation uniquely great to the tyranny of secular values that threaten not only fundamental issues of long-range cultural stability but the very fabric of personal, family, economic, and social strength. This new republic is the environment in which our children will grow and manage their future.

In the early seventies, Francis Schaeffer predicted that this "post-Christian era" would mature into a movement that would become increasingly hostile to believers. His prophecy has come true with uncanny accuracy. As the American culture stretches to become more "open" and "progressive," our proclamations of what is right and true become unwelcome agents of resistance and obstruction to the architects of this cultural change. In one of his book titles, Schaeffer asks, "How Shall We Then Live?" For those of us who are aware of the coming of the night in America, this question is of supreme relevance.

The Dawn's Early Light is written to help us know how to live in this new era. It is about thinking Christianly and about living out the truth in a world managed by that which is not true. It is about right-side-up living in an upside-down world. This book is not about mere *survival* in our increasingly hostile culture, but rather it is about *success*. It is about conquering the darkness with the power of the light.

Clearly this is not a time for despair. It is a time to join the overwhelming majority of God's people who through the centuries have found their faith and the living proclamation of truth from their lives to be a threatening irritation to the cultures in which they lived.

As a church and as individuals, we must now refocus our strategy. The political wars we have fought are an important front in the battle. They will finally fail, however, if we in this hour do not allow God to bring about a transforming spiritual revival in our lives. This is the only weapon that will win the battle between light and darkness.

The Scriptures tell us that God is light. As He is ignored or resisted within the various institutions of our society, darkness will pervade and grow. Yet the Scriptures also say that He gives us the ability to let His light shine through us by the way we live. If this generation will live according to the biblical principles outlined herein, I believe that what appears as dusk turning to darkness could actually be the first rays of a new dawn.

It is my prayer that as this book is read it will be used of God to equip us for persistent faithfulness until righteousness prevails or until He returns to usher in His grand and glorious reign.

ACKNOWLEDGMENTS

Books are like plays. Even though the actors are seen, critiqued, and sometimes applauded, dozens of others go unnoticed behind the scenes. Without their commitment, the play could not be staged. A brief notice in the playbill or a quick flash in the closing credits hardly seems an appropriate way to recognize their contributions.

Such is the case with *The Dawn's Early Light*. Special thanks goes to Ken Durham for helping to condense some sections of this work from spoken to written form. His labor was strategic. My secretary, Betty McIntyre, is to be commended for her oversight of the typing of the manuscript. Andrea Miller graciously assisted Betty.

I owe thanks also to Don Johnson, Dennis Shere, Greg Thornton, Bill Thrasher, and others at Moody Press who believed in this book and patiently yet urgently encouraged me to the completion of this project. I am grateful as well to my editors, Cathy Norman and Anne Scherich, who skillfully put mind and hand to the final form of the manuscript.

Needless to say, this book would not have been possible without the loving support of my wife, Martie.

Writing a book is something like giving birth. A concept springs to life deep in our souls. It grows cell upon cell. It is nourished, nurtured, and constantly changes until, through labor and travail, it is finally born—to live and be productive in its lifetime.

Although the work of all who have made the birth of this book possible is over, it is our prayer that the Spirit will now use the book's message to ignite a quiet revolution that will ultimately prevail against the darkness. May our Lord grant it to be so for His glory and the advancement of the cause of Christ.

1

THE DARKNESS DEEPENS

The Place and Power of the Light

It was a chilling experience to read the *Newsweek* cover story about the advancing gay and lesbian rights movement.[1] It was chilling for many reasons. Whereas the radical, hostile elements of the movement were discussed, a large segment of the feature surveyed gay and lesbian couples who were portrayed as upstanding members of the community, rearing children and claiming rights as legitimate American families. No credible space was given to a balanced view of those who oppose the imposition of homosexuality as an alternate life-style on our culture. In fact, in the closing paragraph this question was posed: Is it possible that those who oppose this movement are like the racists of the sixties who opposed civil rights? The article referred to those who struggle against the movement as "homophobics."

It's a new day when speaking out against sin is a slur against "civil rights" and righteousness is a cultural phobia. America has changed its mind, and our new republic is showing its stuff at every turn.

For years, Christians in America have watched and wondered as this dramatic and devastating shift has taken place before our eyes. It has marched across our headlines, seduced our media, claimed its day in our courtrooms, subtly won over unsuspecting people, voiced its precepts from wayward pulpits, and platformed our politicians.

Daniel Yankelovich begins his book *New Rules: Searching for Self-fulfillment in a World Turned Upside Down* with a penetrating metaphor. He observes:

> According to the geological theory of plate tectonics, giant "plates" undergird the earth's surface and keep it stable and rigid. Sometimes these immense geologic formations, grinding against one another beneath the surface of the earth, shift their positions. Their movements may be slight, but the plates are so massive that along their fault lines even slight shifts cause volcanoes and earthquakes on the surface. Increasingly in recent years, our studies of the public show the "giant plates" of American culture shifting relentlessly beneath us.[2]

The shift seems nearly complete, and as the dust settles, the changes on the surface are profound.

In a recent Supreme Court ruling regarding the Christmas manger scene on city hall lawns, the majority, represented by Justice Blackmun, concurred that America is to be ruled as a secular state.

Everything is fair game in our educational system. Our children are exposed to satanism, and health classes endorse "alternate sexual life-styles"; yet God and biblical values are at best ignored and at worst banned from the classroom.

Many politicians believe they can't get elected without the support of abortionists and sodomites.

A public library's three display cases are used for municipal groups to display their causes. It grants space to the gay rights group in town but refuses space to the pro-life movement.

The slaughter of innocents continues with legal protection.

In most states a teenage girl must still get parental permission for an aspirin from the school nurse, yet she can get an abortion on the advice of a school's health center without her parents' knowledge.

The legalization of drugs is seriously discussed as a valid option by politicians, leading influence peddlers, and educators.

A CBS news commentator publicly apologizes for legitimate comments made about homosexuals after meeting with leaders of the gay rights movement.

A "pro-life" governor in Idaho vetoes a pro-life bill after great pressure is brought to bear by abortionist groups who threaten a nationwide boycott of Idaho potatoes.

We have watched, wondered, and worked. Yet in spite of our work, which is like attempts to stem the tide with a pitchfork, a "new day is dawning." But it is the "dawning" of night. That which was right is wrong, and that which was wrong is now often right. Those values and principles that made our nation great are by and large culturally despised. And those of us who claim the unchanging authoritative values of God's Word as our only direction for life suddenly feel left out in the cold. Disenfranchised. Threatened. Sometimes intimidated. Sometimes fearful. Sometimes angry. Often confused.

What must we do?

Shall we fight to regain the ground? Although every effort is worth the pain, it may well be too late to reclaim this culture for biblical values. It is a hollow and tentative gain to legalize values if the culture has no heart for them. We must pray. We must work. We must voice our perspective, though it may soon be little more than the voice of one crying in the wilderness.

Indeed, we have fought a good fight. We have had our day in the sun. Throughout the late seventies and early eighties, presidents claimed to be born again. The evangelical presence was felt from the cover of *Newsweek* magazine[3] to the halls of Congress. National office holders believed they could not get elected without the evangelical bloc. The Moral Majority movement was an influence peddler. Everyone knew our name and felt our presence.

Then, surprisingly, just when we thought secularism was a toothless tiger, it rose up and powerfully reversed a Supreme Court nomination. Jerry Falwell resigned from the leadership of the Moral Majority. Right-wing religious leaders publicly shamed the cause. Gay rights bills were passed in nearly every major American city. The radical feminist, pro-abortion, and pro-homosexuality lobbies gained ground and now hold phenomenal power. Pro-life politicians began tasting defeat, and political wisdom confesses that it's hard to get elected while opposing abortion. The new secularism is now boldly promoted on talk shows, and Christian values are ridiculed on prime time sitcoms, which promote tolerance of a looser, "progressive" culture.

Christian consensus in our land is gone. We may have lost the day. Across the land there is a growing feeling that we are up against formidable odds and, given the strength of the secular momentum, apart from miraculous intervention there is little hope of reclaiming the day. More and more leaders are quietly admitting that the tide may be irreversible. Chuck Colson states that there is a "growing sense of despair and defeatism in evangelical ranks that I've witnessed around the country." He goes on to say, "In a mere decade the 1980's moral majority has become the 1990's persecuted minority." A prominent evangelical veteran of the battles of the '80s told Colson he was through. "Why bother?" he confided privately.⁴

Although we need to continue to fight it out in the political arena, we are now at a time when we must refocus our strategy. In fact, it is time to start reclaiming the most powerful weapon we have against the darkness. A weapon that seems to have suffered as we have picketed and politicked as though revival comes through governmental power. This weapon is the weapon of individual proclamation of light. Light, in Scripture, is the penetrating, revealing, unquenchable force of a personal expression of rightness and truth. It is ignited not through public policy statements but rather in and through individual lives that are nonnegotiably committed to thinking and living from a biblical point of view. The light of righteousness is always superior to darkness and ultimately prevails. It carries more long-lasting power and influence than public policy or political gain. In fact, governmental cultural gains are empty and ultimately doomed without the clear, uncompromised presence of the personal expression of light through our lives.

Actually, there is evidence that during the last twenty years, while we temporarily gained political ground, we lost ground in our personal uniqueness as the light of the world.

Rodney Clapp observes, "North American evangelicals are now acutely awake to the fact that they live in a post-Christian culture. There is much talk against violence, sensuality, and materialism. Yet even the most casual observer can see that the evangelical church is 'infected badly' by all three."⁵

In his book *Twilight of a Great Civilization* Carl Henry observes,

We are so steeped in the anti-Christ philosophy—namely, that success consists in embracing not the values of the Sermon on the Mount but an infinity of material things, of sex and status—that we little sense how much of what passes for practical Christianity is really an apostate compromise with the spirit of the age.

Our generation is lost to the truth of God, to the reality of divine revelation, to the content of God's will, to the power of His redemption, and to the authority of His Word. For this loss it is paying dearly in a swift relapse to paganism. The savages are stirring again. You can hear them rumbling and rustling in the tempo of our times.[6]

Whereas we thought we were gaining, we have suffered significant losses in the way we as Christians think, process cultural input, react to everyday situations, and live. Under the surface of all the political clamor, secularism has stolen our minds and, consequently, our hearts.

Whether we ever gain the political presence and power again is secondary to the pressing need to be uncompromised light in the darkness. In fact, neither Scripture nor history demonstrates that political advantage accomplishes true spiritual gain, either personally or culturally. Christ called us to the power of productive personal righteousness when He said, "You are the light of the world. A city set on a hill cannot be hidden. Nor do men light a lamp, and put it under the peck-measure, but on the lampstand; and it gives light to all who are in the house. Let your light shine before men in such a way that they may see your good works, and glorify your Father who is in heaven" (Matthew 5:14-16).

Now is the time to challenge the deepening darkness and begin to penetrate the night with the light of a new dawn. We must dare to challenge the night with the weapon of a life undauntedly committed to rightness.

As we refocus our strategy that we might be productive and effective lights for Christ in this hostile environment, three commitments are necessary to empower and make effectual the work of the light.

COURAGE

Christ's words in Matthew 5 indicate that those who penetrate the darkness with light do not hide it under a basket. Instead, they lift the light high on a lampstand. It takes courage not to be intimidated by the darkness of a culture that so powerfully and loudly promotes non-Christian values. It takes courage to stand undaunted when we feel outnumbered, rejected, and isolated in basic assumptions and beliefs. It takes courage to know we are right when so many influential people say we are wrong.

It's no wonder God said to Joshua when he was about to enter the hostile environment of the land of Canaan,

> Only be strong and very courageous; be careful to do according to all the law which Moses My servant commanded you; do not turn from it to the right or to the left, so that you may have success wherever you go. This book of the law shall not depart from your mouth, but you shall meditate on it day and night, so that you may be careful to do according to all that is written on it; for then you will make your way prosperous, and then you will have success. Have I not commanded you? Be strong and courageous! Do not tremble or be dismayed, for the Lord your God is with you wherever you go. (Joshua 1:7-9)

Joshua's courage was to be founded on the bedrock of living according to the righteousness of God's law and the assurance of God's presence, light, and power for life in an opposing culture.

Actually, Christianity in its uncompromised, authentic form has been most often planted in hostile environments and has thrived in the midst of opposition. In the pre-Christian history of the Old Testament, Abraham and his family were led by God to inhabit the land of the Canaanites, where Sodom and Gomorrah were located and where the highest statement of allegiance to Canaanite gods was the blood sacrifice of children on altars of stone.

Christ Himself ministered in an intensely antagonistic, apostate setting and in an environment ruled by the decadent Roman Empire. It was the surprising alliance of this religious and political atmosphere that led to the redemptive murder of our Lord.

In the New Testament, churches were planted in desperately wicked cities, such as Ephesus, Corinth, and Rome. Many of the apostles were violently terminated for their faith.

Throughout history, the pattern flows through every generation as God's people accepted, without flinching, the challenge to light the darkness with the righteousness of their lives. Even today, in places such as South and Central America, China, and until recently Russia and the Eastern bloc, the church faces great cultural oppression. Recently, in Africa, as nationalism flourished and governments demanded a return to the spirit worship of their forefathers, unflinching deacons and pastors were buried neck deep with stakes pounded through their skulls as a warning to others who would not comply. Idi Amin butchered thousands of Christians in his bloody reign in Uganda.

Quite frankly, we in America have enjoyed an unusual season of grace. It is not normal for the work of Christ to exist and thrive in friendly climates, or to see the church at work in an agreeable context. Nearly all the biblical metaphors for the church suggest contrast and conflict. Light in darkness. Soldiers in warfare. Athletes in training, striving to conquer.

So, then, who are we to claim and cling to the unusual privilege of living with cultural support? History and even our present demise demonstrate that Christians rarely thrive in contexts that even partially support the values of righteousness. As Isaac Watts so correctly wrote:

> Must I be carried to the skies
> On flowery beds of ease,
> While others fought to win the prize,
> And sailed thro' bloody seas?
>
> Are there no foes for me to face?
> Must I not stem the flood?
> Is this vile world a friend to grace,
> To help me on to God?
>
> Sure I must fight if I would reign;
> Increase my courage, Lord;
> I'll bear the toil, endure the pain,
> Supported by Thy word.

PERSISTENCE

By focusing our strategy to be unquenchable light in the darkness, we must be committed not only to courage but to perseverance as well. It takes time for the light to penetrate and for the darkness to bring about decay and ultimate despair. Yet courageous persistence in righteousness ultimately wins the day for the light. Scripture teaches that whereas righteousness always brings its reward, unrighteousness ultimately pays in debilitating consequence. As the light dawns in the darkness, as rightness produces its positive results and sin cultivates its consequence, in time the contrast will become dramatic as the light prevails in winsome contrast to the deepening despair of darkness.

Consider the outcome of godlessness. Scripture affirms, "There is a way which seems right to a man, but its end is the way of death" (Proverbs 14:12). The more unrighteous values are actualized, the more devastation, despair, and death in human terms will be realized. Think of the outcomes:

- AIDS and venereal disease will continue to increase. Even now, a study at Stanford University declares that it is possible for a partner to contract five strains of venereal disease in one sexual encounter.
- There will be a decreasing sense of worth and value as life becomes cheaper, guilt becomes heavier, and women become more degraded and victimized through pornography and the resultant crimes of rape, violence, and abuse.
- Disorientation of families will increase as children are reared in day-care centers, gay and lesbian partners are regarded as families, single parent homes become more and more prevalent, and things transcend the value of people—children, in particular.
- Personal financial pressure will continue to create more interpersonal tension as the lust for gain is fanned by easy money, fast credit, legalized gambling, and the availability of expensive comforts and convenience.
- Lives will become increasingly enslaved and wasted on pornography, alcohol, drugs, gambling, and other substances that addictively destroy productivity and potential.
- A subtle form of anarchy and judicial confusion will no doubt prevail as everyone does what is right in his or her own eyes.
- Whereas pleasure will abound, happiness will continue to be the elusive dream. Satisfaction over the long term will become more and more unattainable.
- Business will suffer as the employee base becomes composed of people committed to pleasure, greed, and self-satisfaction

rather than a work ethic, loyalty, and the satisfaction of leading a productive life.

• Quick pleasure will give way to long-range brokenness and loneliness as self-fulfillment pays its ultimate dues.

Godlessness always delivers its consequence. History, personal experience, and Scripture affirm, "Do not be deceived, God is not mocked; for whatever a man sows, this he will also reap. For the one who sows to his own flesh shall from the flesh reap corruption" (Galatians 6:7-8).

Paul lists the profile and results of godlessness:

> But realize this, that in the last days difficult times will come. For men will be lovers of self, lovers of money, boastful, arrogant, revilers, disobedient to parents, ungrateful, unholy, unloving, irreconcilable, malicious gossips, without self-control, brutal, haters of good, treacherous, reckless, conceited, lovers of pleasure rather than lovers of God; holding to a form of godliness, although they have denied its power; and avoid such men as these. For among them are those who enter into households and captivate weak women weighed down with sins, led on by various impulses, always learning and never able to come to the knowledge of the truth. And just as Jannes and Jambres opposed Moses, so these men also oppose the truth, men of depraved mind, rejected as regards the faith. (2 Timothy 3:1-9)

Yet, as the psalmist clearly states, "Do not fret because of evildoers. Be not envious toward wrongdoers. For they will wither quickly like the grass, and fade like the green herb" (Psalm 37:1-2).

By contrast, persistent righteousness pays *positive* life outcomes. David opens the book of Psalms with this declaration:

> How blessed is the man who does not walk
> in the counsel of the wicked,
> Nor stand in the path of sinners,
> Nor sit in the seat of scoffers!
> But his delight is in the law of the Lord,
> And in His law he meditates day and night.
> And he will be like a tree firmly planted
> by streams of water,

> Which yields its fruit in its season,
> And its leaf does not wither;
> And in whatever he does, he prospers.
>
> (Psalm 1:1-3)

Paul follows the profile of godlessness with encouragement to adhere to what is right, regardless, in 2 Timothy 3:10-17:

> But you followed my teaching, conduct, purpose, faith, patience, love, perseverance, persecutions, and sufferings, such as happened to me at Antioch, at Iconium and at Lystra; what persecutions I endured, and out of them all the Lord delivered me! And indeed, all who desire to live godly in Christ Jesus will be persecuted. But evil men and imposters will proceed from bad to worse, deceiving and being deceived. You, however, continue in the things you have learned and become convinced of, knowing from whom you have learned them; and that from childhood you have known the sacred writings which are able to give you the wisdom that leads to salvation through faith which is in Christ Jesus. All Scripture is inspired by God and profitable for teaching, for reproof, for correction, for training in righteousness; that the man of God may be adequate, equipped for every good work.

We must know, however, that our courageous persistence to stand firm will be challenged by the inevitable cultural backlash as we live righteously.

Peter, writing to a church living under the persecution of a hostile environment, underscored the vital role of the light of righteousness as he encouraged Christians under pressure to "keep your behavior excellent among the Gentiles." The verse goes on to say that as we claim the ground of good works, we can expect to be slandered "as evildoers" (1 Peter 2:12).

On a recent trip to the East Coast, I was listening to a talk show discussing people like me who claim life as a sacred commodity and therefore oppose abortion as a means of disposing of unwanted babies. The hosts and callers agreed that people like us are evil. They said we are like the fascists of World War II, wanting to control other people's lives, and that if we were to win on the issue of abortion, we would go on to seek to control other private areas of their lives. They claimed that we were against their inalienable rights. We want to keep women subservient, risking their health by encouraging coat-hanger abortions and robbing them of the privilege of governing their own bodies. All who talked and called agreed. No one spoke out for righteousness. I felt the same sense of bewilderment and isolation as when the *Newsweek* article likened me to a racist for opposing homosexual sin as a legitimate alternative in our land.

Peter said we would be slandered "as evildoers." If that were all Peter could promise, I suppose we could recoil and take the hit as maligned martyrs. Yet he goes on to project a glorious and victorious prospect. We should so act that "they may on account of your good deeds, as they observe them, glorify God in the day of visitation."

When visitation from God, their judgment, comes upon them (which is inevitable), they will note the stability and success of our lives, and the light will draw them in and cause them to give credit to God and righteousness. Although this verse may have application to the ultimate visitation of God in judgment, there are many times in Scripture when God has visited judgment upon present sin. The word *visitation* literally means when God draws near. Sometimes it is in the form of individual suffering for the consequence of sin; sometimes it is God's visitation on a person, a family, a culture, or a nation.

This, then, is the effect of the light. When the darkness unravels in the despair of its own judgment, the light rises at dawn as a victorious alternative. As we persist unintimidated, the quality of our lives, families, finances, relationships, and businesses becomes a more powerful statement than even the imposition of political power or legislated morality.

In essence, the day will come when people will turn from the despair of the darkness and notice the distinctive difference in our lives. As the epidemics of AIDS and venereal disease become more widespread, our lack of affliction will be noticeable. Whereas no one has a perfect home, homes that hang together and follow God's basic patterns for the family will stand in diametric contrast to the widespread disintegration of the American family. The sense of fulfillment and lifelong stability and security that righteousness brings will draw attention in a world that increasingly finds these commodities personally inaccessible. A commitment to biblical stewardship will produce financial freedom, and freedom from the enslaving influence of alcohol, drugs, pornography, and gambling will be clear evidence of the superior nature of the light.

In *Newsweek*'s special edition on AIDS, the predictions as to serious loss of health are sobering:

> The U.S. epidemic has always been concentrated in major cities, among gay men and IV drug users. But that pattern is changing as the epidemic matures. Last year AIDS incidence rose nearly four times as fast in the nation's smallest cities as in its largest ones. And while the number of new cases rose by 11 percent among gay males, it increased by 36 percent or more among heterosexuals and newborns. . . . Syphilis and gonorrhea—diseases that not only indicate unsafe sexual practices but facilitate the spread of the AIDS virus—have skyrocketed in recent years. At the same time, the crack epidemic has created a whole new class of high-risk heterosexuals: women who trade sex directly for the drug. "We've seen the rate of syphilis in various parts of the country quadruple because of sex associated with crack," says Don Des Jarlais of the Chemical Dependency Institute at New York's Beth Israel Hospital. "The same thing could happen with AIDS."[7]

The article states, "Monogamous couples are not at risk." That's the power of light in the darkness. Yet the sentence concludes, "But there's no evidence that Americans are about to become wholly monogamous." That's the stubbornness of the darkness.

It must be recognized that righteousness does not guarantee exemption from trouble. Living as a part of a fallen race means that even the most committed torch bearer could contract AIDS from a transfusion. Godly people at times have children who rebel. Remember that Cain and Abel came from the same home. Those who are unalterably committed to the light may lose their jobs for that commitment. What now is the effect of the light?

Actually, it is in affliction that the light shines most brightly. In the early church it was the patient loving response to persecution on the part of believers that confounded the world and caught its attention. When trials come our way, people start to notice us and, more significant, to notice how we respond. As Hebrews 10:32-33 says, "Remember the former days, when, after being enlightened, you endured a great conflict of sufferings, partly, by being made a public spectacle through reproaches and tribulations, and partly by becoming sharers with those who were so treated."

The King James states that we become a "gazingstock" in our world. Given the riveted attention that our lives attract in affliction, our "good works," the light through our lives, present a dramatic contrast to the response of those in dark similar situations.

Having contracted AIDS innocently, instead of bitterness and hate toward those who have caused it, a loving, active, compassionate response toward drug users, homosexuals, and other AIDS victims in the Spirit of Christ demonstrates the unique power of the light. When children rebel, embarrassing us and causing considerable pain, instead of alienating and holding wayward children hostage to our vengeful response, the light shines as we love unconditionally and stand like the father of the prodigal son, waiting to welcome and forgive. There is power in the right when the light shines through in our steady response to a job loss, as we show that our security and supply is not in a job but in the provision of God.

Light in affliction means responding righteously. Hatred, revenge, self-pity, rebellion, slander, anger, and all the other dark responses to trials are inconsistent with the light. Love, forgiveness, compassion, courage, patience, and other uniquely biblical responses are what fuel the light in our lives.

For Shadrach, Meshach, and Abed-nego, it was their undaunted commitment to rightness that led them into the fire. In that fire, the light of their testimony of unintimidated persistence and their preservation by God led the king of Babylon to decree that their God was indeed the only true God (Daniel 3). The light of their good works in the midst of trouble led the king to glorify God and to dismantle the darkness of idolatry.

I asked a Russian pastor why he thought Gorbachev had lifted the oppression from Christians in the Soviet Union. He replied that the major problem facing Russia is its faltering economy. Much of the trouble, he explained, is due to absenteeism, alcoholism, and nonproductivity in the work force. Gorbachev reportedly told Russian leaders, "Why do we oppress the very people who do not absent themselves from work, who are not alcoholics and who give us a productive day's work? We need their strength." It was the light of a *persistently righteous* community of repressed Christians in a hostile culture that finally, in the day of economic visitation, caused the light to be seen and God to be glorified. As a result, today Bibles are freely distributed, evangelism is taking place in homes and stadiums, and Christians are free to worship without interference. In fact, Russian business leaders have asked Westerners to help them establish the values of the Ten Commandments that they, too, might know stability and success.

It is no wonder that Joseph and Daniel rose to places of great influence in pagan lands. They were reared with an undaunted commitment to truth, and they persistently practiced righteousness. The quality of their lives made profound statements in the face of the lack of personal quality that the dark paganism of Egypt and Babylon produced.

One of my most rewarding experiences in the pastorate was baptizing a couple who had accepted Christ because they had watched their neighbors model biblical values in their home. They asked one day, "What makes your family work so well?" Soon after, they received Christ and began to infuse their home with biblical light.

The rallying cry of the Latins was *carpe diem*. It meant "seize the day." This cry must be ours today. Scripture calls us to seize the day for Christ. We must penetrate the darkness with the unquenchable rays of a dawning personal righteousness that reclaims our lost minds and hearts and reflects the authentic power of historic Christianity, uncompromised by the cultural shift. Now is the time to learn what it means to "be careful how you walk, not as unwise men, but as wise, making the most of your time, because the days are evil. So then do not be foolish, but understand what the will of the Lord is" (Ephesians 5:15-17).

This is our season to actualize Christ's words "Let your light shine before men in such a way that they may see your good works, and glorify your Father who is in heaven" (Matthew 5:16).

AUTHENTIC RIGHTEOUSNESS

In our commitment to courageously persist against the night, it becomes imperative that we have a clear understanding of authentic righteousness, particularly in terms of the key issues that the darkness has redefined and used to quietly seduce us, in effect extinguishing our light. For example, what is the righteous standard for commodities such as success, prosperity, and purpose in life? What does the light dictate about people and our relationships? Is there a distinct ethic regarding trouble that the light brings to a culture addicted to peace and comfort? Do we have a heart of compassion toward even the worst and most aggressive supporters of the advancing darkness? We don't need the issues of homosexuality, abortion, drugs, violence, and illicit sensual fulfillment defined again; there is a consensus among us as to the wrongness of these demons of the dark. Rather, the insidious, subtle, almost unnoticed capitulation to attitudes and actions in our basic understanding of fundamental issues of life will ultimately rob us of our power and position in this culture.

It begins in our mind. We must learn to think authentically righteous thoughts about the basic commodities that surround us and drive our existence. Bringing our minds under the authority of His Word, instead of this culture's, and permitting our lives to be transformed by the renewing of our minds are the keys to challenging the darkness with the light of His truth in us.

It may well be that the simple words we sang as children "This little light of mine, I'm going to let it shine" are more profound today than we had ever dreamed.

NOTES

1. "The Future of Gay America," *Newsweek*, Mar. 12, 1990.
2. Daniel Yankelovich, *New Rules: Search for Self-fulfillment in a World Turned Upside Down* (New York: Random, 1981), p. xiv.
3. Kenneth L. Woodward, John Barnes, and Laurie Lisle, *Newsweek*, "Born Again! The Year of the Evangelicals," October 25, 1976, pp. 68-70, 75-78.
4. Chuck Colson, "From a Moral Majority to a Persecuted Minority," *Christianity Today*, May 14, 1990, p. 80.
5. Rodney Clapp, "Remonking the Church," *Christianity Today*, August 12, 1988, p. 20.
6. Carl Henry, *Twilight of a Great Civilization* (Westchester, Ill.: Crossway, 1988), p. 15.
7. "AIDS: The Next Ten Years," *Newsweek*, June 25, 1990, p. 21.

2

THINKING

Igniting the Light in the Night

In a large metropolitan area, an evangelical pastor is arrested in connection with a series of brutal rapes, stretching over several years. Though his friends and parishioners insist that he could not be guilty, within a few days he confesses to all charges. He says it all began with his addiction to pornography.

In another city, a bitter split within a conservative Protestant church results in lawsuits and litigation that leave deep wounds, much bitterness, and a congregation that no longer ministers or reflects the love and mercy of Jesus Christ.

All across North America, countless couples divorce and in so doing elevate statistics for "Christian" divorce to a level equal to that of non-Christians. Likewise, recent polls reveal that so-called "social drinking" and alcoholism among professing Christians is nearly equal to that of unbelievers. More widespread and subtle, yet equally damaging, is the reality that Christians often think, act, and react according to the standards of the fallen world, which extinguishes our light and eliminates our uniqueness. Everywhere we turn, in fact, we find that the way Christians think about the world bears a striking resemblance to the way the world thinks about itself.

Like the proverbial frog boiled to death in a pot of water that has been ever-so-slowly heated, many in this generation seem to have become so gradually secularized that we barely recognize the difference between that which is secular and that which is sacred. And it all begins in the way we think.

DARK FOOTPRINTS OF SECULARISM

Secularism leaves dark footprints everywhere. From abortion to gay rights to immorality, this nation no longer seems able to distinguish right from wrong. A firm standard of righteousness no longer sets the pace. Now the pace is set by the one who shouts the loudest, lobbies the longest, pays the most high-powered lawyers, or rises to stardom and fame.

That might not be so bad, except that we know life is not worth living without God and apart from the direction of His Word. We are only beginning to pay the tragic price of secularism as the fundamental commodities of our society deteriorate and disintegrate. Secularism is destroying our homes, health, happiness, and harmony.

On some fronts, the church valiantly rises to stem the tide. We march against homosexual "rights," we lobby for life and infiltrate the political process. We decry the decadent, prayerless humanism of our schools; we denounce the deceit and subversion of secularists who fight dirty for their anti-God agenda. We've declared war on the New Age movement, and we condemn the media when it displays an anti-Christian bent.

But as important as all that is, we have failed to guard against an even greater danger. We have not realized how insidiously the poison of secularism has contaminated our way of thinking. We who advocate the purity that Scripture affirms unashamedly entertain ourselves with much that is impure. Things that would have once caused alarm in our spirits are now tolerated and even enjoyed. We who are repulsed by homosexuality, adultery, and drunkenness can easily become neutralized and open to the demands to use words like "gay," "affairs," and "substance abuse" to describe sin.

We are instructed to shine as lights in the darkness, but we must determine whether our own minds have already lost their luster. The pivotal question is, Has the world changed our minds for us?

If it has, we have already lost. No march, picketing, lobby, or political process will mean anything if God's people have no light. That light begins with the way we think. The fact is that God has —and has always had—a standard of righteousness revealed in His Word. It is not first a standard for righteous behavior; it is a standard that begins in the way we *think*. Unfortunately, the pressures and seductions of our secular society have caused many in the Christian community to abandon that which is right and accept the wayward standard of secularism.

Although we are diligent to campaign for sweeping changes in behavior, we lose more and more mental ground to the world system. We've been talking for years about *behavior*, but the real battleground is *the mind*. We can't appropriately talk about right moral codes and right laws until we have first disciplined our minds to think sacredly instead of secularly.

This will be the Christian battleground into the next century. If we are to claim great victories for Jesus Christ, we must first reclaim the Christian mind. We need to learn to think rightly in a world gone wrong. For, as a man "thinks within himself, so he is" (Proverbs 23:7).

FROGS ON THE ROAD

"Dad, watch out for the frogs on the road!" Little Emily bolted to her dad's shoulder with the urgent announcement of impending danger.

"Frogs?" her father replied. "What do you mean?"

"That sign back there," she said. "It said, 'Caution, frog area ahead.'"

Her father laughed and said, "Emily, the sign said, 'Caution, fog area ahead.'"

Emily indignantly insisted, "I know my letters, and I know my words. That sign said frog area ahead." To prove her point, she spelled it out: "Frog—F-O-R-G!"

Her mind was made up. As far as she was concerned, she was right and her father wrong. For the next several miles, she devoted her energy to watching for green, slippery, hopping frogs on the turnpike. The way she thought determined her responses. On the other hand, her father had read the sign correctly, recognized the real danger, and kept his eyes open for fog clouding the highway.

Two people in the same car, on the same road, having read the same sign managed their lives from two entirely different perspectives. Each had processed the data, made a decision, and acted accordingly.

There's no doubt that the way we think determines the way we live. Our lives are shaped by the way we process the information around us and determine what our perspectives, opinions, and responses will be. What we are today is the sum total of all the thoughts we have permitted to lodge in our minds, shaping the way we live. Our thoughts affect specific immediate decisions and actions and influence general life patterns and life-styles.

In a way, the fog episode in Emily's car is a microcosm of a most significant issue: how are we going to interpret life's information and make our decisions? Throughout our lives, the way we read the "street signs" will determine the way we form practical judgments and decisions, which, in turn, direct and determine the course of our lives—and ultimately our eternal destiny.

CONTROLLING OUR THOUGHTS

Since living begins with thinking, it is essential that we control and discipline our thought process. Minds that fly on "automatic pilot" usually fly according to someone else's flight plan. In fact, minds that are not under the Holy Spirit's control are minds that quickly fall prey to the schemes of our adversary and his destructive power.

1 Corinthians 2:14 tells us that a "natural man"—the person who does not know Christ—"does not accept the things of the Spirit of God; for they are foolishness to him, and he cannot understand them, because they are spiritually appraised." This man is in the dark spiritually, and his life decisions are nothing more than the best of his own thoughts.

On the other hand, this passage reveals that "he who is spiritual appraises all things, yet he himself is appraised by no man. For who has known the mind of the Lord, that he should instruct Him? But we have the mind of Christ" (vv. 15-16). In other words, the Christian has a great advantage because he is equipped to think biblically, that is, to formulate and apply operational conclusions that are thoroughly biblical, ultimately and absolutely correct. It is the "mind of Christ," or God's Word, that sheds God's light on our natural darkness. It alone can instruct us in how to think accurately and biblically.

The third chapter of 1 Corinthians begins with Paul's statement that he couldn't speak to his audience as spiritual men but as "men of flesh, as . . . babes in Christ." Why? Because although they were equipped to think biblically, they were not doing that. And as a result, they were stuck in spiritual infancy and were dangerously indistinguishable from the world around them.

FROM THE CRADLE TO THE CRUCIBLE

What does it mean to think? What processes develop our understanding and definitions for life?

Actually, thinking begins at the most basic level. As infants, not much matters to us except being fed, being dry, being held, and getting plenty of sleep. At that stage of life, our responses are more or less passive and instinctive. Not much thinking is required.

This nonthinking stage of life soon gives way to the thrilling adventure of independence and self-determination. As we move on to crawling, exploring, and elementary forms of communication, thinking becomes critical and begins to shape our behavior. As every parent knows, most of our thinking at this age can be characterized by the words "me" and "mine" and other forms of self-indulgence and self-interest.

As we mature and grow in this crucible called life, our experiences become more sophisticated and complicated. From deep within us comes the desire for popularity, power, success, peace, prosperity, pleasure, pleasing relationships, and purpose. We begin to look for ways to extract fulfillment and satisfaction from life. These needs and longings fuel our momentum, preoccupy our minds, and establish the direction of our lives.

In *Alice in Wonderland*, Alice asked the Cheshire Cat, "Would you tell me, please, which way I ought to go from here?"

The Cat replied, "That depends a good deal on where you want to get to."

"I don't much care where," answered Alice.

"Then," said the Cat, "it doesn't matter which way you go."

The way we mentally define, manage, and control our passions ultimately directs the quality of our lives.

FORMING "OPERATIONAL CONCLUSIONS"

The emergence of desires requires new commitments in our lives. Whereas infancy was passive and instinctive, independence and self-determination are ruled by *how we think*. The way we think plays the central strategic role in how we seek success, pleasure, peace, prosperity, and all the other basic desires of life. It determines whether we are effective for Jesus Christ or simply "spacers" in the pews on Sunday morning. Our thinking determines whether we will experience the radical, abundant life He offers us or simply mimic the world around us and suffer the consequences.

Paul recognized the basic necessity of biblical "operational conclusions" when he prayed for the Colossians. He knew that their responses and decisions would begin with and result in knowledge of God: "that you may be filled with the knowledge of His will in all spiritual wisdom and understanding, so that you may walk in a manner worthy of the Lord, to please Him in all respects, bearing fruit in every good work and increasing in the knowledge of God" (Colossians 1:9-10).

Nothing is more crucial than the "operational conclusions" we reach in life. They determine whether we live with the fantasy of frogs in the road or see life accurately. They create illusions and self-deception, or they enable us to live life gloriously with results for Christ and His kingdom.

For instance, when you see a sign that says "Success" along the road, how do you read it? If previously your operational conclusion defined success by cars, boats, salary, who you know, where you live, where you go, prestige, and power, then that kind of operational conclusion will determine the course you take to reach "Success." Likewise, the way you interpret the signs that direct you to peace, prosperity, popularity, or purpose will determine the means you use to reach those destinations.

Unfortunately, the operational conclusions or practical judgments of many Christians today are being determined not by the Word of God but by the world around us. Therefore, it is the first job of every believer to read the signs correctly and to form operational conclusions that are accurate, biblical, and ultimately beneficial.

USING OUR "MARVELOUS MECHANISM"

Now that we understand the importance of our life-directing conclusions, we need to understand the process that determines our operational conclusions. What is thinking, and how do we arrive at life's decisions?

Thinking begins in a piece of equipment called the brain. The brain is a marvelous product of divine engineering. Encased in a protective shield of bone and skin, the brain is surrounded by highly technical instruments built to provide essential data. Eyes, ears, nose, mouth, and a sophisticated nervous system send continual input to the brain through delicate cords that, like wires in a computer, carry messages that are logged, cataloged, retained, or discarded.

A miracle of supernatural technology, the human brain has more circuitry than the largest computer network in the world. Every second it is deluged with more than a hundred million separate messages. It unconsciously responds to most of those messages while shutting out or ignoring those that are irrelevant.

If I force myself to think about other stimuli as I write this manuscript, I become aware of noisy machinery in the background. I can also make myself aware of my fingers feeling the press of the pencil and the weight of my legs against the chair. Yet as I write, I am consciously aware of none of these things. The impulses to breathe, move, swallow, pump blood from my heart through my veins, and even to marshal healing agents for a recent cut in my foot are all managed automatically by my brain while I concentrate on the message of this book. No other sound or feeling is relevant to my concentration, so my brain blocks out other stimuli, and I can focus on my task.

Soon hunger signals will stimulate the desire to refuel for the afternoon. All of this is processed through one hundred billion nerve cells (neurons) that form one hundred trillion separate connections, each capable of representing a single bit of information. Recorded on paper, that information would fill twenty million volumes. To make use of the entire storage capacity of one brain, a person would have to learn something new every second for ten million years.

Although everyone has this marvelous mechanism, clearly no one even begins to approach its vast potential. As staggering as the possibilities may be, the real challenge is not *how much* of our brain we use, but *how* we use it.

STEPS IN THE THOUGHT PROCESS

Essentially, there are three fundamental steps in the thought process. These are: *gathering data, deliberation,* and *discernment*. Let's examine each one and determine how together they determine the way we think and live.

GATHERING DATA: THE WAREHOUSING OF FACTS AND PERCEPTIONS

Before adequate conclusions about life can be reached, the mind must gather the appropriate facts to begin the thought process. The mind serves as a colossal warehouse for storing life's data. Thinking is built upon a complex foundation composed of facts about what is hot and what is cold, mathematical formulas for addition, subtraction, multiplication, and division, colors, names and faces, historical facts of personal and public experiences, time, deadlines, and thousands of other facts. From elementary facts such as "That is a tree," to complex facts about nuclear fission, the more information we have, the more accurate we can be about life and the better equipped we are to reach truly good, beneficial conclusions.

By nature, man possesses a certain hunger for data. For some young children, counting to one hundred provides an early thrill. Throughout our lives, the joy of discovering new facts fuels the mind's hunger for information. Even the author of Ecclesiastes admitted that "wisdom excels folly as light excels darkness" (2:13).

Most critical to the gathering of facts is the guarantee that the "facts" we store are true and not misperceived. A student came to me one day and said that he had seen a Porsche® turn the corner in front of him with the license plate "MBI-1." If he hadn't checked with me, he might have assumed the "fact" that the president of Moody Bible Institute drives a Porsche! In every area of life, we must not only determine what is fact, but we must also patiently wait until we know enough about a situation to trust the reliability of the information. This means that the facts we collect throughout our lives need to be carefully checked.

This is where the Word of God becomes an essential tool for the Christian. The Bible presents itself as the final measurement for all data—that is, truth—concerning every area of life. We are assured in 2 Timothy 3:16-17 that "all Scripture is inspired by God and profitable for teaching, for reproof, for correction, for training in righteousness; that the man of God may be adequate, equipped for every good work." God's Word guarantees facts about relationships, Christ, eternity, history, people, money, the world around us, and the universe beyond us.

Therefore, what we log as "fact" in our minds must have a reliable source that can be checked against misperception and be in concert with the objective standard of Scripture; otherwise, false data will distort our lives and perceptions. Gathering and guaranteeing facts —true, reliable data—is the foundation for thinking accurately.

DELIBERATION: VALUES AS VEHICLES

As I was growing up, my mother tried to prepare me for life by urging me to make up two things: my bed and my mind. When I got up each day she would remind me, "Joe, make up your bed." And when I couldn't decide what I wanted to buy or eat or do, she would prod me, "Joe, make up your mind."

Making up my mind over the years has proved to be the most significant activity in my life. From friends, to a marriage partner, to a calling, to the temptations that come my way every day, making up my mind has made up the essence of my life.

Making up our minds is a matter of processing information according to our own beliefs and values. Just as each of us has a brain, each of us has the capacity to think. But the real issue is not whether we *can* think; it's whether we think *correctly*. Correct thinking leads to correct conclusions—to those operational conclusions that guarantee a high quality of life. Unfortunately, correct thinking has eluded the modern Christian. Because of the overwhelming influence of our secular culture, our process of deliberation has been corrupted by values that have their source in the fallen world rather than in the Word of God.

Values, in fact, are the key. They are the vehicles that enable us to organize facts to form our conclusions and behavior. Values give meaning to the facts we accumulate. They determine what significance we attach to facts. For example, if it is a fact that apples cost $5 each, the "value of frugality" may lead me to deny the purchase of an apple. On the other hand, if I value the pleasure of eating an apple more than frugality, I might go ahead and purchase an apple. Or again, if one apple is the last piece of food available during a famine, then the "value of survival" will far outweigh the injustice of a high price.

Along a more relevant vein, if I value personal happiness and pleasure above all else, then I will reach one conclusion about abortion. If, on the other hand, I value life as a sacred priority, then I will make quite another decision.

Our values are the filter through which all information passes during the thinking process. Values are pivotal, but they vary. They change with time and differ from culture to culture. As a child, you may have valued red and blue as a beautiful combination of colors, but now you may be partial to earth tones or pastels. It took me twenty years to value asparagus and spinach as table fare.

On a trip to West Africa I was surprised to learn that a man's status was not determined by the way he dressed. It did not matter whether he wore finery or rags. It did not matter if he wore jewelry and gems. Instead, his status and worth was determined by how his wives dressed. Was he wealthy enough to dress them in finery, including the best fabrics, jewels, and precious metals? If so, he was a man of means and rank. (Actually, that's not far from our culture, except that in our culture we men like to dress expensively, too.)

Another value in that area of West Africa is that the larger one's wife is, the more beautiful she is. In fact, a local proverb says, "If your wife sits on a camel and the camel cannot stand up or breaks its legs in the process, then she is truly a beautiful woman." That value has led some husbands to force-feed their wives just to make them more "beautiful." When we compare the West African culture to ours —where thin is "in" and a slender wife is a prize—it is obvious that some values are not universal.

Where do we get our values? Values are instilled in us by our families, our experiences, our teachers, our heroes, our culture, our community, our socioeconomic group, and our entertainment media. As Christians, however, it is imperative that we adopt our values from God's infallible Word, the Bible, and place a higher value on what

God says is right than on what the world says is acceptable or what our "want to" dictates.

Our values must be biblically based if we are to reclaim our minds for Christ. Whereas some values are a matter of preference, such as choosing books over sports, other values are absolute and are clearly taught in Scripture. In direct contrast to our culture's values, authentic Christian values regard people above possessions, others above self, eternity above the present, righteousness above the temporary pleasure of sin, His will above my will, forgiveness above revenge, giving above receiving, children over careers, character above credentials, truth above falsehood, fact above feelings, commitment above comfort, and Christ above culture.

Because our values determine how we organize facts and drive us toward decisions, clear biblical values help guarantee a thought process that is godly, beneficial, and eternally significant. All that remains is for the Christian to learn what those values are and to choose them over the prevalent systems of secular thinking and selfish desires.

As a boy, I once sat alone in our car, wondering about the mysterious cigarette lighter in the dashboard. My parents had bestowed their values on me by warning me of the danger. Their values were overridden, however, by my own value system—and the value of curiosity and personal experience won out. I decided that the end of my finger was a reasonable risk. If I had accepted their values above my own, I could have avoided a great deal of pain!

DISCERNMENT: OPERATIONAL CONCLUSIONS IN ACTION

I didn't understand it then, but my thinking process had led me to a decision which, in turn, led to a certain consequence. I never again had to think through that process, at least as it related to metal that glows red. I immediately logged a new *operational conclusion* based on the consequences I experienced. It was "Avoid all that is dangerously hot."

The final step in the thinking process, then, is *discernment*—the capacity not only to make a decision but to make a *correct* decision concerning any given course of behavior. Discernment is a product of the process. If facts are true and not misperceived, and if these facts

are transported to a conclusion by correct values, then we will be able
to discern correct courses of behavior.

Discernment is based on a clear knowledge of right and wrong.
If my thinking process has led to a conclusion that is clearly wrong,
discernment rises to wave the red flag, forcing me either to destruc-
tively disregard the warning or to wisely reevaluate facts and values in
order to produce a godly conclusion and a righteous action. As Hebrews states, the goal of maturity for the believer dictates the development of right decisions (Hebrews 5:11-14).

Thus, thinking is a three-step process that includes data-gather-
ing, deliberation, and decision-making that is checked by *discernment*.
How we manage this process will determine our operational conclusions, which will determine how we live. The thinking that leads to
our conclusions, therefore, must be accurate. Wrong values can lead
to wrong conclusions, in spite of right information. And wrong conclusions result in wrong, unproductive, and even disastrous consequences.

BEWARE OF RATIONALIZATION

Decisions are where value-driven information impacts our lives.
They are important! They are sometimes irrevocable and irreversible,
and they can alter the course of a career, a relationship, or an eternity.

Fortunately, decisions—like data and values—can be checked
against God's Word. The Bible has much to say about actions and
behavior. For example, if I am acting selfishly or foolishly, Scripture
clearly states that my thinking has been fouled, perhaps by wrong
information or wrong values or wrong motives. Hebrews 4:12 tells us
in no uncertain terms that "the word of God is living and active and
sharper than any two-edged sword, and piercing as far as the division
of soul and spirit, of both joints and marrow, and able to judge the
thoughts and intentions of the heart."

But when biblical discernment calls us to reorder our thinking
about our behavior, we must be careful to avoid the neutralizing effects of a thought process called *rationalization*. Rationalization is a
mental excuse that neutralizes productive thinking. It is characterized
by excuses we all have heard or used: "I know it's wrong, but—"; "If
it weren't for the way my husband treats me—"; "I can't help my-

self"; "I know a lot of people who are worse than I am." Rationalization is natural, human, convenient—and wrong.

I am struck by the clarity with which Scripture speaks to this issue. Philippians 1:9-11 reads, "And this I pray, that your *love* may abound still more and more in *real knowledge* and all *discernment*, so that you may approve the things that are excellent, in order to be sincere and blameless until the day of Christ; having been filled with the fruit of righteousness which comes through Jesus Christ, to the glory and praise of God" (italics added). The passage first calls us to restrict our lives to excellent decisions that are the product of a growing commitment to biblical values (in the passage it is called love) in the context of an awareness of true biblical data (knowledge) applied with discernment. The product of this kind of "think-act" is personal and public purity (v. 10), a productive life (v. 11a), and the ability to live out our redemptive purpose of bringing glory to God (v. 11).

What a startling contrast to the way our secular society rationalizes, thinks, and lives!

THE CHALLENGE BEFORE US

The challenge for adherents to authentic Christianity is to be unique in our culture. We must filter life's information through the value system of God's Word, for it produces life patterns, responses, and behavior that are dramatically different from the world's. Living out our biblical value system will create a culture as different from the secular world as West African culture is from North American.

This effectual, authentic, powerful, and unique Christianity begins in our heads, with how we think. And it ends with living out our biblical operational conclusions in pure, godly behavior as lights in the deepening darkness.

Authentic Christians think differently from everyone else. We love and forgive our enemies—not sue them. We display the fruit of the Spirit (Galatians 5:22-23). Our minds are disciplined by the values of Christ, who taught, "You have heard that it was said, 'You shall love your neighbor, and hate your enemy.' But I say to you, love your enemies, and pray for those who persecute you in order that you may be sons of your Father who is in heaven" (Matthew 5:43-45).

Conversely, Christians whose minds remain world-taught and world-saturated act accordingly. They easily hate and seek revenge because their minds have been programmed by pagan operational conclusions.

Authentic Christians think uniquely about success. We define it by such concepts as servanthood, goodness, faithfulness, and eternal gain. When the desire for success rises within us, our conclusions will drive us to act biblically and seek true success by serving others, being faithful, and making an impact for Jesus Christ. We will live to hear our Savior say, "Well done, thou good and faithful servant," the ultimate statement of success.

By contrast, secularized Christians' minds continue to be enslaved by the false world system. When they desire to succeed, they will place above all else such things as houses, cars, power, position, and earthly prosperity. They will live for the things the Bible says "moth and rust" will "destroy, and . . . thieves break in and steal" (Matthew 6:19).

It is no wonder that when Christ prayed that His own would survive their pilgrimage in a hostile, satanically controlled system, He asked, "I do not ask Thee to take them out of the world, but to keep them from the evil one. They are not of the world, even as I am not of the world. Sanctify them in the truth; Thy word is truth" (John 17:15-17). He was praying, in essence, that His children be guarded by the truth and that truth would shape their values and guide them toward making beneficial, eternally significant decisions.

The authentic Christian submits his mind without reservation to God and to His Word. He processes information from God's point of view. He lets God's values become his values. He makes biblical decisions without wavering, compromising, or rationalizing. And he courageously persists in penetrating the darkness with God's powerful light.

God said through the prophet, "My thoughts are not your thoughts, neither are your ways My ways" (Isaiah 55:8). Left to ourselves, we will fail. But the good news is that the life-changing power of a new way of thinking is not only a necessity but a joyous experience in victory. Paul commanded to "not be conformed to this world, but be transformed by the renewing of your mind, that you may prove what the will of God is, that which is good and acceptable and perfect" (Romans 12:2).

3

BRAINWASHED

Transiting from the Secular to the Sacred

Psychologists tell us that more than ten thousand thoughts go through the average human mind in one day. That's 3.5 million thoughts a year. According to medical experts, sitting up in bed increases one's energy requirements by 10 percent, standing nearly doubles the energy need, and chopping wood increases one's energy needs nearly eight times; however, heavy thinking requires hardly any extra energy at all.

Why is it that our minds process some three and a half million thoughts every year, but we give so little thought to thought itself? Could it be that we fail to realize what's at stake? The Bible reminds us that as a man "thinks within himself, so he is" (Proverbs 23:7), which means that our lives are the product of the way we think.

Veteran diamond cutter Adrian Grasselly studied the 155-carat Liberator diamond for two full months in 1944 before he ever laid a chisel to the stone. It was the largest diamond ever found in Venezuela, and one wrong move would instantly have ruined the $200,000 investment. But because he took time to think through every move, Grasselly fitted his chisel into a groove, rapped it with a steel bar, and successfully began the process of moving a priceless diamond from rough stone to finished gem.

In many respects we are diamonds in the rough, and as such we should discipline and train our minds to think through carefully the moves we make, in order to avoid ruining the vast potential God has placed there.

Junk Food for the Brain

In preparing for a speech on nutrition, my high school son Matt discovered that in order to receive the U.S. government's recommended daily allowance (U.S.R.D.A.) of thiamine, a person would have to eat 12.5 Ding Dongs® per day. The U.S.R.D.A. for niacin would require 59 McDonald's® chocolate shakes, or 100 Chicken McNuggets®, or five bags of Cheetos®, or 10 Pop Tarts®. The minimum requirement for protein would mean eating 25 Twinkies®. He concluded that you really are what you eat.

Even more significant is the fact that we are what we *think*. Just as it is inconceivable that anyone could receive the nutrition he or she needs from massive doses of junk food, so it is inconceivable—by biblical standards—that anyone could receive the mental and spiritual nutrition he needs by ingesting massive amounts of the world's programming day after day and year after year.

Similar to junk food—tasty and fun but of little value and ultimately damaging—are the secular messages sent to our brains en masse every day. Take, for example, the message offered by a recent television ad campaign: "Success is getting what you want; happiness is wanting what you get." To the average listener (Christian or non-Christian) this pleasantly presented axiom is tasty, pithy, memorable—and classic junk food for the brain. The "principle" stated in the axiom is diametrically opposed to Scripture. Yet if we hear the message often enough, before long we may find ourselves not only believing it but living it out like all the pagans around us.

This is but one example of hundreds of junk food thoughts offered us every day. In fact, if we ever hope to think correctly about the danger of receiving "junk thoughts" from the world system, we need to understand that during the past decades North America has changed its mind dramatically. Culturally, it has moved from thinking patterns based on Scripture to a decidedly secular pattern of thought.

Intellectually, it has rejected thinking processes based on objective biblical evidence to foregone conclusions that automatically exclude the supernatural. Philosophically, it has moved away from the concepts of truth, morality, ethics, and virtue toward the belief that there are no absolutes and that everything is relative.

Unfortunately, the way Christians think has moved, too.

A Strategic Assault

At the birthday party of a friend who had just turned fifty, I noticed the napkins imprinted, "Of all the things I've lost, I miss my mind the most." As light as that statement was in that context, I could not help but wonder if the same could be said of the church: Of all the things we've lost in the past three decades, we miss our minds the most. Of course, the problem is not that we are mindless; it's that we've lost our minds to a world dominated and directed by satanic misinformation and non-truth. Our adversary's assault on our minds is as much a threat to our stability, security, and success for the kingdom as would be the most vile crime or most powerful mind-altering drugs. Satan knows that if he captures our minds, he owns our lives and futures.

Consider, for example, Satan's motive behind the great Babel project of Genesis 11, where he unified the minds of all peoples (except for a remnant of Shemites) under one manner of thinking, one world philosophy, one social religion, and one language. It was so powerful a strategy that God Himself declared that if it should be allowed to continue "nothing which they purpose to do will be impossible to them." Satan's goal, of course, was to defeat the plan, purpose, and people of God. His strategy was to capture the minds of all so that without thinking they would submit to the world system with one voice ("Come, let us . . . "; v. 3).

Although God frustrated Satan's purpose by confusing man's language, Satan's strategy has not changed. If he can capture our minds and bring them into subjection to unified popular thought, or the world's way of thinking, then his strategic assault has won the day. He knows that influencing our minds strikes a tactical blow to the cause of Christ.

As Paul reminds us, our warfare is not against flesh and blood but against an entire hierarchy of demonic power and influence managed by Satan (Ephesians 6:10-18). Satan's objective is the defamation of God's glory, as well as our destruction because we are statements of God's glory. Moreover, the more he does to get us to disparage God's name and defame God's reputation, the more individuals he will be able to keep from entering the kingdom. To render us ineffective as Christians is to render us useless as witnesses for Jesus Christ.

Consider for a moment what the media-magnified events of the past few years have done to the effectiveness of our Christian witness in North America. In light of televangelists who have "fleeced the flock," preachers who have given in to immorality, and phony faith healers, has it become easier to lead a lost person to Christ or more difficult? Are your neighbors more open to the gospel or more closed than they were ten years ago? Obviously, capturing the minds of even a handful of influential, visible, newsmaking Christians has served Satan's battle plan effectively.

Is it any wonder that the first piece of armor mentioned in the warfare warning of Ephesians 6:10-18 is the weapon of *truth?* Truth is the ultimate power against the invasion of false thinking. Remember that Peter called us to "gird [our] minds for action" (1 Peter 1:13). Any understanding of spiritual warfare that ignores the battlefield of the mind is tragically misguided and doomed to fail. It is an oversight that we simply cannot afford to make.

British scholar Os Guinness tells a story about the problem of theft in Russian factories during Nikita Khrushchev's reign that makes a similar point. When an outbreak of petty thefts from factories threatened the Soviet economy, guards were placed at the exits of each factory to search the workers at the end of the day. In Leningrad, every evening a worker pushed a wheelbarrow containing a burlap bag full of wood chips and sawdust past the guard. Every evening the guard would inspect the bag, and every evening he would find nothing of consequence. After a week of this ritual, the guard could stand it no longer. He pulled the worker close and pleaded, "Tell me, comrade, what you have been smuggling past me every night. I swear I will not turn you in!"

The worker leaned close and whispered, "Wheelbarrows."

Like the guard distracted by a burlap bag while the real theft took place right under his nose, the church in North America has become so focused on material and political issues that the real problem—the secularization of our thinking—has continued to spread unhindered.

THE FIRST ATTACK

Note that, in the beginning, the most devastating attack from Lucifer was directed against the human mind. Eve, living in the midst of all the pleasures of Eden and enjoying unhindered love and fellowship with God, as well as with Adam, was intercepted by the serpent. Satan's goal was to gain dominion over creation by capturing the allegiance of the divinely appointed governors of creation, Adam and Eve (Genesis 1:26-27). But first he had to change the way Eve thought about God, her environment, and herself. If he could control her mind, he could control her will and ultimately her future.

His first volley was to convince Eve to change her mind about God, to think incorrectly about God's goodness. God had already told her, "From any tree of the garden you may eat freely; but from the tree of the knowledge of good and evil you shall not eat" (Genesis 2:16-17). No doubt Eve perceived God as generous and was thankful for His abundant provision. After all, He had given her access to all but one tree in her world.

Enter the adversary, who sneered, "Indeed, has God said, 'You shall not eat from any tree of the garden'?" (Genesis 3:1). Suddenly, God no longer seemed generous. He seemed stingy. Just think of it— He would not let her eat of every tree in the garden! Eve began to change her mind about God. She began to question His goodness.

Next, Satan led her to think wrongly about God's trustworthiness. Satan slyly whispered, "You surely shall not die! For God knows that in the day you eat from it your eyes will be opened, and you will be like God, knowing good and evil" (Genesis 3:4-5). Eve probably began to wonder, *Who can trust a God who misleads you for His own benefit?*

The adversary then led Eve to think differently about her environment. No longer was the Garden to be tended and enjoyed as an act of love and faithful stewardship toward God. Rather, the Garden became a place that could bring benefit and glory to Eve. In fact, she reasoned, she could be like God, if she would eat. Of course, that would mean disobeying God, but why should she obey God who (in her mind) was neither good nor trustworthy?

Not only was her mind changed about God and her environment, but Eve also began to think differently about herself. Life was
no longer a matter of loving and glorifying God herself but rather of
loving and glorifying herself with what God had created. "When the
woman saw that the tree was good for food, and that it was a delight to
the eyes, and that the tree was desirable to make one wise, she took
from its fruit and ate; and she gave also to her husband with her, and
he ate" (v. 6).

THE FALL AND FALSE LOGIC

Once Eve had changed her thinking about God, and the data and
the values in her personal world had been reordered, she reached a
decision—an operational conclusion—that allowed her to eat what she
knew had been forbidden. She sinned, and Adam sinned with her.
They became secularized in a very modern sense. And, in that moment, Satan gained dominion over mankind and over all creation.
When Satan changed Eve's mind, he changed her world.

But what does Eve's experience have to do with the way we think
and live our lives today? We don't live in Eden. To the contrary, you
and I live in a world that suffers the effects of Adam and Eve's sin.
With every thought and decision, we experience the consequences of
Satan's seduction of Eve.

This, in fact, is the link between Eve's situation and ours. One
theologian has astutely distilled the thought process of that first sin
down to its basic logic, and we can see that it is the same false logic we
employ every day.

Major premise: Restrictions are not good.

Minor premise: God's plan is restrictive.

Conclusion: God's plan is not good.

Too often we make decisions based on that operational conclusion. And too late we look back and realize that we were duped by the
first premise—the one our culture screams at us from every front:
"restrictions are not good."

Today we live in the wake of the liberal juggernaut of the "siz-
zling sixties," that era in North America that convinced our culture
that restrictions in any form are bad and that limits should be taboo in
a "free" society. We have heard that mentality proclaimed so often in

ads, sitcoms, movies, and even in soft drink jingles that we have, perhaps unknowingly, come to believe it.

THE FATHER OF LIES

Why was Satan able to so thoroughly deceive Eve? Jesus Christ revealed Satan's credentials when He said to the Pharisees, "You are of your father the devil, and you want to do the desires of your father. He was a murderer from the beginning, and does not stand in the truth, because there is no truth in him. Whenever he speaks a lie, he speaks from his own nature; for he is a liar, and the father of lies" (John 8:44).

Satan lied to Eve, and he is still seeking to capture our minds through the same basic lies. His entire battle plan is managed and directed by distorted data and false values, which, in turn, lead to us to make erroneous operational conclusions. And though the players and the setting have changed dramatically since that first "mind assault" in the Garden of Eden, the stage and the strategy are the same. Satan still assaults us with doubts about God's goodness and trustworthiness, and about the nature and purpose of our existence and the world around us.

The lies of Satan permeate every facet of our society. Find in Scripture something that God has declared as true, and somewhere in our society you will find an overwhelming contention that it is *not* true. For example, the Bible clearly establishes that man was personally fashioned by God as the climax of creation. Our culture, on the other hand, teaches that man is a genetic accident, an animal in the process of mutation. Scripture teaches that mankind has been given stewardship of all animals. Some animal rights activists, however, proclaim that animals are equal to man. God's Word teaches that man and woman are distinctly different. Our culture, meanwhile, attempts to erase that distinction. God teaches that we exist to bring pleasure to Him. Satan's system teaches that we exist to bring pleasure to ourselves. And so it goes; wherever God provides right thinking for us, the world repeatedly and continually tells us just the opposite, because Satan is the driving force behind the world system.

THE SHIFT TO THE SECULAR

Ultimately, the entire belief system of our society teaches that the world, its people, and its treasures are here to use for the enhancement and glory of *ourselves*. The idea that we are to use the world around us to enhance and glorify God is totally foreign. And it's tougher now to do that than ever before. A steady movement toward the secular in America's mind has elevated destructive thinking to unprecedented levels of acceptance.

During the past forty years in North America, our values and operational conclusions have dramatically shifted. At one time, our culture was governed by a consensus of Judeo-Christian thought, though even then society was no less sinful at its core. But at least life was regarded as sacred, homes were honored and secure, homosexuality was clearly viewed as wrong, and God and the church were outwardly revered.

With the onslaught of relativism (the belief that there is no right or wrong, but all is relative) and an infusion of rationalism (the belief that only that which is capable of being tested and proved is real), we essentially rendered God and His truth useless. At best, God and His Word became irrelevant; at worst, they became a hindrance to "progress." The Humanist Manifesto II declared God to be "harmful." We began to publicly order our lives by nonbiblical, godless, faithless values. In turn, our present secular society evolved.

PAGAN VALUES

The prevailing philosophy we call secularism is now the primary value in our culture. Secularism tells us that if God *does* exist, He is irrelevant and we need not integrate Him into the mainstream of life, thought, or intellectual pursuit. Belief in God is something to be laughed at or laughed off. Any demand God may make on our lives is dismissed. Occasionally our culture may tolerate a token tip of the hat to His existence, and faith may provide some strength and comfort in times of trouble, but otherwise God is a nonissue.

Secularism is self-proclaimed to be "open-minded," tolerating the serious consideration of any belief—as long as it's not "religious." Therefore, humanism, evolution, witchcraft, and other false systems can be considered in schools and other settings without interference.

But God, or talk of God, is regarded as offensive and inexcusable. Secularism relegates God to church buildings and aggressively separates itself from a worldview in which God is the prime Mover and Sustainer of all things.

In a world where God's existence is not acknowledged, the new rule of existence is the rule of man and is based on his own wishes, his own wisdom, and his own moral code. Unless our values are shaped by a higher authority—that of the Bible—believers are in danger of processing the data of life according to the same secular, godless point of view.

Without doubt, it is incredibly dangerous for Christians to live without turning to God's authority and Word as we form our thoughts. Surely the psalmist recognized this when he wrote, "How can a young man keep his way pure? By keeping it according to Thy word. . . . Thy word I have treasured in my heart, that I may not sin against Thee" (Psalm 119:9-11). Without daily, conscious accountability to God, even our life-styles will become indistinguishable from the world's.

The dominance of secularism has given rise to its own set of values that leads to distorted and destructive operational conclusions. These values are vehicles that have led to the formation of new rules for living in a secular society, and they replace the Word of God as the standard and pattern for right and wrong. There are, in fact, at least four dominant cultural values that contradict God's truth and pollute clear, authentic, productive Christian thinking and living.

NARCISSISM

Predominant among secularism's false values is narcissism. Narcissism is the notion that life should revolve around me and claims that I am the greatest entity in my personal universe. All that really matters are my rights, my privileges, my happiness, and my prosperity. Other people are always secondary. Loving myself and looking out for "number one" are all that matters.

Predictably, the more we think according to this pattern, the worse our lives become. As life's information enters our brains, it is filtered through our "me first" values and then organized and translated into decisions that we think will benefit us. This "Don't tread on me" mentality eventually destroys families, relationships, work habits, ethics in the marketplace, church unity, and community stability. Even believers are not exempt from falling into this thinking: "It's time I did something for myself. It's time to do what *I* want. I'm tired of living for God and for everyone else."

The result of self-dominated thinking is the destruction of relationships and alienation from others and God as we lock out everyone else and barricade ourselves within a ghetto of one. By contrast, God values giving ourselves away to Him and to others (Matthew 22:34-40).

HEDONISM

Hedonism is secularism's lie that life is to be lived solely for pleasure. Popularized by the Playboy movement born during the relativism of the late 1950s and '60s, hedonism claims that there are no limits to seeking pleasure. And since personal pleasure is the goal of life, all information processed by the brain leads to conclusions that are directed toward fun, thrills, and good times.

Hedonists, for example, assess abortion in light of what feels good to the mother—what will bring her immediate pleasure, relief, or happiness. The hedonists' motto is a mixture of "If it feels good, do it" and "Let your glands be your guide." Thus, hedonism fans the destructive flames of pornography while diminishing the value of women and making them merely objects of male pleasure. It promotes homosexuality and contributes to the spread of sexually transmitted diseases, such as AIDS and syphilis. It replaces responsible living with a "thrill at any cost" approach to life. Hedonistic attitudes have been the undoing of many successful marriages and happy homes. It has bound many with the destructive cords of addiction to lust.

Unfortunately, those who think that pleasure is the supreme end of life can suddenly find themselves broken, lonely, and sad. We must not forget that our adversary's desire is to destroy us (John 10:10*a*; 1 Peter 5:8). God, on the other hand, values the pleasure we find in our allegiance to Him (Psalm 149:4; 2 Corinthians 5:9).

PLURALISM

Pluralism is the cultural belief that there are many right ways to live and believe. There are no absolutes, so there's nothing to be dogmatic about. Find whatever works for you. If it's Jesus and Christianity, great. If it's Hinduism, that's great, too. Islam, Shintoism, Judaism . . . whatever. Like narcissism and hedonism, pluralism blossomed from the seeds of relativism and claims to free man from the limitations of absolute truth and the imperatives of the Word of God.

Pluralism is the religion of our college and university campuses, where it aggressively militates against any belief in the God of the Bible as the source of absolute truth.

Pluralism reduces convictions to convenient opinions and makes dogmatism an outdated approach to life and experience. It may sound compassionate and reasonable to parrot pluralism's sentiments: "All paths lead to the same god," or, "God wouldn't turn away sincere people." But the fact is that those attitudes contradict the clearly non-pluralistic statement of Jesus Christ when He said, "I am the way, and the truth, and the life; no one comes to the Father, but through Me" (John 14:6). This is the same truth Peter proclaimed to the religious leaders when he declared, "There is no other name under heaven that has been given among men, by which we must be saved" (Acts 4:12).

Unfortunately, Christians who have been seduced by pluralism no longer say, "Thus saith the Lord . . . " or, "The Bible says. . . . " Instead, we say, "It seems to me . . . " or, "It's not for me, but I'm glad it works for you." Yet the psalmist claims that the laws of God are *right* (Psalm 19:8). Scripture is clear that there is a right and wrong and that we will personally be held accountable.

MATERIALISM

Materialism may well be our culture's most prominent value. It reduces life to the sentiment "I am what I have" or "I can be happy if I get . . . "

Instead of making that which is spiritual and eternal life's top priority, materialism elevates that which we can see, touch, taste, smell and, most important, possess to the place of greatest prominence. Children, spouse, health, church, the Great Commission, and even God become secondary to the ultimate value of the accumulation of things. Few values could be more destructive.

Perhaps those who display the motto "The one who dies with the most toys wins" are trying to be clever, but in reality the motto has been the undoing of many lives. People by the millions invest their lives amassing the latest of everything, and when they die have worse than nothing. Christians who buy into materialism—as perhaps the majority do today—eventually put their commitment to Christ on the back burner.

TRANSCENDENCE AND THE NEW AGE

We can see that secularism and its values leave a spiritual void in lives that are, by God's design, incurably religious. Therefore, even though the world's system is steeped in an anything goes, "me first," "pleasure first," "things first" mentality it still must offer some kind of transcendent experience. Enter the New Age movement.

Few philosophies in Western history have made a more profound impact on the thinking processes of a nation, especially in relation to individuals' concept of God. The New Age movement encourages any who seek a transcendent experience to think of God merely as a depersonalized force that exists in each of us. New Age thinking promises that the seeker can discover this force, tap its resources, and then use its power for his or her own benefit. This force does not impose any ethical standards. The only personalization occurs when we "realize" that because this force is in us and in everything around us, we ourselves can be gods.

The prevailing idea is that this force is here for us—not that we are here for it. It claims to offer the same god that every other religion worships. Sin, hell, heaven, redemption, justification, and sanctification have no part of New Age thinking.

The claim that we can be gods, of course, is nothing new. In Genesis 3:5 the serpent promises Eve that if she eats of the fruit, "you will be like God." Offering man equality with God and escape from accountability for sin are some of Satan's oldest and most effective strategies. And they continue to work today.

The trouble with New Age thinking is that viewing God as the generic "power base" of the universe leads to disastrous conclusions. Life and religion become no more than self-serving mystical experiences.

It is vital to drive home the truth that each of these secular values is diametrically opposed to God's values. As opposed to the self-serving mode of narcissism, biblical values require that I give myself to God and to the good of others. When Christ was asked about the greatest command, He replied, "'You shall love the Lord your God with all your heart, and with all your soul, and with all your mind.' This is the great and foremost commandment. And a second is like it, 'You shall love your neighbor as yourself.' On these two commandments depend the whole Law and the Prophets" (Matthew 22:37-40). Hedonism is countered by the privilege of living to bring pleasure to God through living justly, loving mercy, and walking humbly with our God (see Micah 6:8). The absolute rightness of God in all He says, does, and is requires a rejection of pluralism and the materialistic mind-set of our culture. Christ teaches us to live for the things of eternal value by seeking first the kingdom of God (see Luke 12:13-34).

THE THOROUGHLY SECULARIZED MIND

As we approach the twenty-first century, secular values and their consequences will continue to saturate our society. They are everywhere—in our schools, corporate training programs, commercials, counseling, TV dramas, cartoons for kids, music, and the front page news. They threaten to seduce every Christian mind.

I once counseled a couple by showing them clearly from Scripture that changes were needed in their relationship. However, as they left it was clear that the biblical principles I had cited were not an option for them. Though both had been raised in Christian homes, they had been so deeply affected by secular society that they placed their own pleasure and convenience above the authority of the Word of God.

What about Christians who leave marriages simply because they're not happy? What about Christians who are so eager to accumulate material things that they become too busy for God and family or who are too deeply in debt to underwrite the work of the kingdom? What of Christians who feel that God is "an important part of my life" but can't say He is their supreme authority?

We may well have lost our minds. Rather than practicing consecrated thinking, many of us are greatly influenced by the values and definitions of our secular culture. When we lose our minds, that is, when we fail to appropriate and employ the "mind of Christ" (1 Corinthians 2:16), we lose our way and become vulnerable to the disastrous plans of the adversary.

Even more tragic is that we are on the threshold of losing our children as well. While our generation struggles to oppose the advancing values of secularism and stem the tide, we are slowly losing our purity through countless "small" compromises. We give up ground a yard at a time, yielding to the "little" issues: sensual entertainment, questionable language, off-color jokes, shady business practices, lukewarm commitment to Christ, and a dozen other compromises.

As we wander from Scripture and lose our focus, we become more selfish, more pleasure seeking, less adamant about truth and its authority, and more committed to possessions. As a result, our compromises become our children's commitments. Already the next generation is being bombarded by secular values through music, media, and peer influence. Our homes may well be the last stronghold where we can promote authentic thinking and living. It is imperative, therefore, that through example and instruction we create an environment in which biblical information, values, and decisions are preeminent and uncompromised.

Reclaiming Lost Ground

Like soldiers in a battle, our first priority as believers should be to reclaim the ground we have lost to the enemy. We need to be "brainwashed" in the best sense, cleansed by the truth of the Word of God so that our definitions, values, and operational conclusions are in line with His will—not our culture's secularism.

Remember the Corinthians? They were believers who had been thoroughly inundated by the secular culture around them, and they had a hard time breaking free from that influence. So after reminding them who would *not* inherit the kingdom, Paul told them, "Such were some of you; but you were washed, but you were sanctified, but you were justified in the name of the Lord Jesus Christ, and in the Spirit of our God" (1 Corinthians 6:11). That was what they needed to know in order to begin thinking Christianly, so they could regain the ground they had lost to the secularism of their day.

In order to counter secularism's negative influence on Christian marriages, Paul reminded another group of believers that "Christ . . . loved the church and gave Himself up for her; that He might sanctify her, having cleansed her by the washing of water with the word, that He might present to Himself the church in all her glory, having no spot or wrinkle or any such thing; but that she should be holy and blameless" (Ephesians 5:25-27).

It is for good reason that we are urged: "Present your bodies [that includes our minds] a living and holy sacrifice, acceptable to God, which is your spiritual service of worship. And do not be conformed to this world, but be transformed by the renewing of your mind, that you may prove what the will of God is, that which is good and acceptable and perfect" (Romans 12:1-2).

Jesus said that we must be sanctified, set apart, and made unique by the truth (John 17:19). Biblical truth is the filter through which all information, deliberation, and decisions must be processed. Only God's truth can accurately and authoritatively reject false values and distinguish that which is true.

An addiction to God's truth will change our minds, our lives, and our future.

4

THE POWER TO CHANGE

The Worth, Work, and Wonder of the Word

A Texas rancher, in Germany visiting farms and studying European agriculture, asked a German farmer, "How big is your farm?"

The German replied, "Well, it's a quarter of a mile long by a quarter of a mile wide." Then the German asked the Texan, "How big is your farm?"

"Oh," said the Texan, "if I get in my pickup truck when the sun comes up, I can drive all day until the sun goes down and not leave my ranch."

The German shook his head sympathetically and said, "Yes, I had a pickup truck like that once, too."

Whether it's our perspective on personal tastes or on life itself, one of the most difficult things to change is the way we see things.

OBSTACLES TO CHANGE

What makes change so difficult?

Undoubtedly, one obstacle to change is age. I'm not very old, but I have to admit that already I feel the calcifying effects of age around the fringes of my life—a hardening of the arguments, if you will. I'm a little less tolerant than I used to be. My opinions are a little more difficult to change. Another viewpoint—sometimes even God's —is a little tougher to see and understand. My system of life is well-rehearsed, so when someone comes along and suggests change, it is becoming increasingly difficult to react objectively. Yet change is the essential ingredient in becoming uniquely righteous. A classic example of living to change others is the story of a Dutch couple who had been married for fifty years, yet had fought every day of their marriage. They had lived for fifty years in misery, each partner refusing to change. It was that old marriage standoff: she said that when he changed, she would; and he said that when she changed, he would.

The couple's children threw a fiftieth wedding anniversary party for them. After the anniversary celebration the elderly woman, by then in an unusually mellow mood, turned and said to her husband, "Dear, we've lived together for fifty years, but it's been miserable. We've fought every day. Now I think it's time to change. In fact, I've been praying that it would change. I've been praying that the Lord would take one of us home. And when He answers my prayer, I'm going to go live with my sister in Grand Rapids." We're not supposed to change by demanding that others change around us.

We encounter other obstacles to change as well. We may be unwilling to consider changes God wants us to make in our lives because of our standard of living. Our morals—or lack of them—may hamper our ability to change. Our pride may be a major obstacle to making life adjustments, especially if we have been vocal in our convictions. Friendships, goals, aspirations, the desire for success, the fear of failure—all can make us resistant to change.

We have to recognize, however, that God expects us to change.

GOD'S REDEMPTIVE PURPOSE

Change, in fact, is at the heart of God's redemptive purpose for us. We know that Romans 8:28 teaches us that "all things work together for good," but do we realize that the "good" is precisely defined in verse 29? "All things work together for good to those who love God, to those who are called according to His purpose. . . . For whom He foreknew, He also predestined to become conformed to the image of His Son." The verses go together. The good that God is working is the process of change. It is directed toward continually bringing us into greater conformation to the image of His Son, Jesus Christ.

In Ephesians 4:11-13, we see that God has given the church gifted servants—evangelists, pastors, teachers, apostles—all for building up the church, until we come into a measure of the fullness of Christ. In other words, we have been redeemed for change so that God might develop character in us. And the development of character demands an ongoing process of change in our lives.

Any of us who says, "I like myself just the way I am," has aborted God's redemptive purpose. On the other hand, when we are willing to change, mature, and be more like Him, God's redemptive plan is at work.

The biblical measure of spiritual maturity is not how long we've been saved or how many spiritual things we've done. Instead, it is determined by how much more like Christ we are today than we were two months ago. God takes pleasure in our lives as we grow to be more like Christ, but to become more like Him we must change—first in the way we think and then in the way we act.

THE KEY AGENT OF CHANGE

What is the key agent of change in our lives? At first glance, perhaps, we could list a whole array of "change agents." We could talk about the change agent of prayer. When I pray, God usually changes more about me than He does about the situation I'm praying for. Prayer is an agent of change in the world around us and an agent of change in our own lives. So if we are going to become more like Him, we need to pray with increasing regularity and intensity.

Preaching also can be an agent of change, depending on our response to it. Are we attentive to those gifted teachers who take the Word of God and penetrate our souls, or is listening to preaching just another religious exercise or biblical event in our lives? Do we come under the proclamation of the Word ready to say, "Lord, change me"? If we do, biblical preaching can be a phenomenal agent of change.

The indwelling Holy Spirit is yet another agent of change. He is a wonderful, penetrating, troubling voice that encourages us to change. The Spirit of God, indeed, is an agent of change when we yield to Him.

The vehicle of change is normally the Word of God. The Bible is our supernatural edge. Without the Bible, we would not know what prayer is, how to pray, or even that we should pray. Apart from the Scriptures, preaching—no matter how forceful or eloquent—has no life-changing authority. And even the ministry of the Holy Spirit in changing our lives is made effectual by the Word He has authored.

In John 17 Christ prays, "I do not ask Thee to take them out of the world, but to keep them from the evil one" (v. 15). He asked the Father to set us apart, to make us unique and useful. By what? The truth. "Sanctify them in the truth," our Lord prayed. "Thy Word is truth" (v. 17).

Thus, the whole process of God's setting us apart to be uniquely used by Him is a process of change, and the key means of that change is the supernatural power of the Word of God.

The Worth of God's Word

No passage more concisely and powerfully underscores the vital role the Word of God plays in our lives than 2 Timothy 3:16–4:2. That passage concludes with the assertion "All Scripture is inspired by God and profitable for teaching, for reproof, for correction, for training in righteousness; that the man of God may be adequate, equipped for every good work. I solemnly charge you in the presence of God and of Christ Jesus, who is to judge the living and the dead, and by His appearing and His kingdom: preach the word; be ready in season and out of season; reprove, rebuke, exhort, with great patience and instruction." In those words Paul clearly lays out the way the Word of God functions to change us.

The passage begins by stating that "all scripture is inspired." Literally, that means that the Scriptures are God-breathed, which underscores the great worth of His written Word. The Bible is the expression of the "breath," or Spirit, of God. In the Bible, God has shared with us the essence of His very being. That gives phenomenal worth to this treasure the Bible.

If God has breathed His Word, then it must be entirely, infallibly consistent with who He is. When we approach the Scriptures, knowing that God is love, that He is holy, and that He cares for us, we can be confident that *everything* written in the Bible is from a God and is consistent with a God who perfectly, lovingly cares for us.

When God tells us how to handle our money, for example, it's not because He wants to rip us off so that He can build a great, eternal kingdom. Rather, His instruction is part and parcel of His character. He loves us, and every expression of His will is rooted in that love and directed toward our greatest good.

God often talks in His Word about forgiveness, self-sacrifice, service to others, and righteousness at all cost. He does so not because He is a cosmic killjoy who wishes to take all the fun out of life—that would totally contradict His character—but because His commands are grounded in His perfect wisdom, justice, and love.

God is wise, and so the Bible is also wise. God is perfect, and so His Book is also without flaw. God is eternal, and so His Word is eternal and never out of date. The list could go on, but one thing is abundantly clear: because it is the expression of His being, being "God-breathed," in every point and in every way, God's Word is perfectly consistent with His character.

Not only does the Bible have great worth because it is entirely consistent with His character, but since it is God-breathed it also carries worth as His supreme authority. God is the divine, sovereign head of the universe. He is God, who spoke to nothingness, and nothingness obeyed and became stars and planets, sky, atmosphere, and living things. He is the sovereign God under whose authority the entire universe operates. He came in the flesh to show us what God is like (John 1:1-8; Hebrews 1:1-3) and as such is the One who spoke to the wind and the waves, which obeyed and became still (Matthew 14:22-33). He is the sovereign, authoritative God. Therefore, our Bible is not a Book with which we negotiate. It is *sovereign*.

This brings us face to face with the enculturated view of authority in many of our hearts today. As we discussed earlier, one of the great problems in the church is that the hearts of God's people have been seduced by a secular culture. We have become secularized in the way we think as well as in the way we live. In our secular society, authority is vested in the individual. Our culture screams, "You are in charge of your universe. You are your own authority." However, in God's view nothing could be further from the truth. God alone is the authority! And His authority is vested in His Word, the Bible.

When I was in the pastorate, a couple came into my office asking for help with a thorny problem they were struggling with in regard to another family in the church. When I heard their story, it was evident immediately that God's Word spoke clearly to the problem. They were dealing with a matter of litigation, and it involved taking another brother to public trial.

We opened the Bible to 1 Corinthians 6 and read what God's Word says. I then explained what some of the biblical alternatives might be for them. We prayed together, and they got up to leave. I said, "Thank you for coming, I'll be praying for you as you seek to apply God's Word to your life." They turned and said, "Well, thank you—but we really aren't sure we're going to do that." For this couple, the Word of God was not authoritative; it was an optional resource.

I'm afraid a lot of us approach the Word of God today as if it were a buffet table or smorgasbord. When I go to a dinner buffet, I like to walk it once to scout out the territory. Then I go back and pick and choose what I like. Tragically, many of us scout out the Word of God for tasty morsels and pick and choose what we want. Then we ignore the rest as though it didn't matter.

God, however, ordained the Word of God to be a divine diet to which we restrict ourselves faithfully, that we might trim off the extra pounds of the flesh and become conformed to the likeness of His wonderful Son. His Word must be our authority. Therefore, we should value the Word and its authority in our lives.

Remember the old E. F. Hutton ads? In a busy restaurant or on a crowded street, someone would turn to a companion and say, "Well, my broker is E. F. Hutton, and E. F. Hutton says . . . " Everyone around would suddenly become completely quiet and listen. Among many Christians, E. F. Hutton seems to get more respect for its advice that the Bible does. Often, in fact, we turn to friends, professional counselors, advice columns, horoscopes, polls, and a dozen other sources for guidance before we consider the eternal Word of God.

My oldest son, Joe, is helping pay his way through college by working as a clerk for a trader on the floor of the Chicago Mercantile Exchange, where futures and commodities are traded. He clerks in the Deutsche Mark pit, where he stands next to the trader—keeping his cards, keeping track when he's long or short, making sure everything is exactly right.

Frequently, Joe and I drive to work together. We sometimes listen to an all-news station and its business report. When the business report comes on, all conversation stops. Joe gets out his pencil and records what the U.S. dollar is worth that day. Why does he do that so faithfully? Because everything he does on that fast-paced trading floor that day hinges on the worth of the dollar.

As potential lights for Christ, we need to open God's Word and remind ourselves daily that everything we do all day long hinges on the worth of His Word. If change will ever come we must value the Book as having supreme worth in our lives—worth because of who God is, what His character is, and what He authoritatively says.

THE WORK OF GOD'S WORD

We have some items of worth around our house that sit on mantles or behind glass doors. Though they may have a good deal of worth to us, basically in terms of function they are worthless.

Yet the Word of God not only has tremendous worth, it also plays an active role in our lives to effect change. Notice its working power as it is "profitable for teaching, for reproof, for correction, for training in righteousness that the man of God may be adequately equipped to do every good work" (2 Timothy 3:16-17).

Business people know what it means to worry about the bottom line. It's time we started worrying about the bottom line of our *lives*. What's the spiritual profit factor in your life? Are your operational conclusions making you profitable in every good work? What is the bottom line in terms of your life's benefit to God's kingdom, eternal values, and treasures in heaven?

The passage in 2 Timothy teaches us that the mechanism that enables us to change our minds from a deficit position to become profitable for God is the Word of God. It teaches us, reproves us, corrects us, and trains us in righteousness.

TEACHING

Let's start with the mind-changing power of *teaching*. We were all brought into His glorious family ignorant and desperately needing to be taught. Having been born naturally into the false system, all we really knew were the ways of the fallen world.

As we have already observed, throughout our lives we have been saturated with false values. We need to be reprogrammed with truth. We need to know God—His will and His ways. We need to know what to do with our time, energy, and money. We need to know what to do with our minds. We need to be taught what to do about friends and how to handle enemies. We need to be taught about family, work, and leisure.

Some might say, "I don't need to be taught about God. I can see God everywhere around me." Psalm 19, in fact, says that the glory of God is revealed in the heavens. When I walk in the woods, I see God. When I see animals, I see God. When I hold a little baby, I can see God.

But how would we know God loves us if His Word didn't teach us? Regardless of other aspects of revelation, His Word teaches us the wonderful truth that He cared enough to die for us. It teaches us specific truth about His character and our relationship with Him. In short, though God has chosen to reveal certain things about Himself through general revelation, we learn things about Him through His Word that we cannot learn anywhere else.

That's how He changes our minds. Through His Word He teaches us truth about who we are, what we should be, and the world around us. He teaches us to change the way we think and the conclusions by which we operate. As a result, He changes our lives that we may be penetrating rays of light.

A few years ago, my wife and I had the joy of teaching the Word of God in Hawaii. It was February, which happens to be when the humpbacked whales arrive. Humpbacked whales are about forty feet long at maturity and weigh about one ton per foot. They carry a thousand pounds of barnacles, and when they jump, or "breach," they extend themselves totally in the air, and then free-fall back into the ocean. You can see the splash five miles away.

During our stay we went out on a whale-watching boat. As we watched the whales jump and play almost within our reach, our guide told us that the whales come down from Alaska every year to calve in the warm Hawaiian waters. Year after year, each family comes back to the very same place around the island. When the calves are born (they weigh about five tons), they are born breech—or tail first. If they were born head first, these air-breathing mammals would drown during the birth process. As a baby whale is born, another humpback whale comes alongside and pushes it up to the surface to help the baby take his first breath of air.

Our guide also told us that the humpback whale sings a "song" that can be heard more than fifty miles away under water. Every one of these whales sings the same song. Each year, the song changes slightly, and every humpback whale in the world will sing that year's song. Amazing! Incredible! What a display of the wonderful creative power of our God!

But after sharing all these wonderful facts with us, our guide said that if we had been here 50,000 years ago, we would not have been able to see the whales because they had not yet evolved from land animals. I could have wept. As I had watched those denizens of the deep, I marveled at what a great and wonderful Creator I have. Those whales showed the glory of God. But our guide, not having read or believed the Word of God, had made up her mind and was sadly wrong about the world she saw. How did I know about the great Creator who had made those whales? The Word of God taught me that all the wonders I see are of God and exist for His marvelous glory. Even greater, that same Word has communicated that God loves me personally and that He has made it possible for me to know Him.

The Word of God teaches us! How hollow and empty to marvel at these humpbacked whales and conclude, "It all happened by chance." God's Word is profitable for teaching, to raise us up from our ignorance and drive us to worship.

REPROOF

God's Word is beneficial not only for teaching but also for *reproof*. Reproof literally means to shed light on something in order to reveal its flaws or problems.

If you've ever had a broken bone, particularly if it was a serious fracture, you were put under an X-ray machine so that the doctor could see the nature of your problem. This is the function of God's Word. It isolates our sin, strips away our rationalization, and exposes our need.

When our children were small we taught them basic, short sections of Scripture that we believed they could apply to their lives. On one occasion, we were caught in a traffic jam going nowhere. It was becoming increasingly evident that we were going to be late for our meeting. My three-year-old son started teasing his little sister in the backseat. Her only defense was to open her magnificent lungs and scream for deliverance.

Needless to say, I was already tense, and I took the folded map I was consulting and "tapped" him on the head to get his attention and to encourage him to "cease and desist." He looked at me with wide eyes and said, "Daddy, it's not 'be ye kind' to hit people." There it was, in Ephesians 4:32, just as we had taught him—and I was reproved. The Word spotlighted my fault and challenged me to change.

We can expect the Word of God to work in our minds during moments of independence and rebellion, as well as in those times of submission and careful study. It will work. It will change our minds by reproving us that the darkness in our lives may be lifted and the light prevail.

CORRECTION

Third, the Word of God *corrects* us. That is a particularly interesting word. When flying to Florida, it seemed to me like a pretty straight shot from Chicago to Fort Lauderdale. But in the cockpit of the airplane is a fine-tuned radar mechanism. All during the trip, the plane is flown on automatic pilot, which continually yet imperceptibly *corrects* the course of the plane to keep it on track. That's what God's Word does for us. It nudges us to keep us on course. It keeps affecting the way we think, the way we draw conclusions, and the way we make our daily life decisions.

A friend of mine tells the story of the time he got on an elevator in a hotel. He was by himself, away from home, and alone in the elevator, when two ladies also got on. They were young and attractive. As he pressed the button for his floor, they said, "Hey, mister—how about a little fun tonight?"

He told me that immediately Galatians 6 came to mind: "[He] who sows to his own flesh shall from the flesh reap corruption" (Galatians 6:8). He said that verse was like a shade drawn between him and what could have been a persuasive temptation. In that moment, the correcting power of the Word of God kept him on course.

TRAINING IN RIGHTEOUSNESS

Finally, the Bible works to train us in *righteousness*. Righteousness is God's divine standard. It is the "right" standard. It is perfect, and it is perfectly consistent with His character.

Yet we live in a society where standards constantly shift and are more often than not contradictory to biblical righteousness. Any so-called standards are set by the majority, the loudest speaker, the most famous, or the latest political action group.

God has a divine standard. Righteousness is about conforming to that standard, the standard that is absolutely true in every situation, all of the time. Because we enter God's kingdom as babes, we need to be aware that the word for training is the same word that's used for child-rearing. We need to be reared to live according to God's standard. In essence, the Word of God parents us. It rears us in righteousness that we might know the standard and live according to it.

Thus, the work of the Word of God is a supernatural, divine work that is designed to change us that we might become light for him, adequately equipped to do every good work. As Matthew 5:16 says, the people in darkness will see the good works that we do and glorify our Father who is in heaven.

Accepting this Book as *the* agent of change in our lives demands that we value its worth and without compromise submit to its work. In this light, regularly reading and learning His Word becomes a strategic part of the process of permeating our world with the light of righteousness.

As we open the Word we should pray, "Lord, this servant of Yours needs to change, and I'm ready to change. So teach me, change my mind about You, about myself, about my world. Lord, reprove me through the Scriptures, let me find something in them that lights my darkness. Correct me, keep me on course, and train me in righteousness. Lord, in that context I now open Your Word. Speak, for Your servant hears."

When we approach God's Word expecting Him to work in us, He will work. Maybe He will do it through a phrase or a chapter. How much we read is not important. What is important is why we read. We should be committed to say daily, "God, here I am, change me."

THE WONDER OF GOD'S WORD

We also need to recognize that this worthy, working, powerful agent is a great *wonder*. Second Timothy 4:1-2 reads, "I solemnly charge you in the presence of God and of Christ Jesus, who is to judge the living and the dead, and by His appearing and His kingdom: preach the *word*" (italics added). The *Word*. Scripture and experience teach us that it is a Book of supernatural wonder.

The Word of God is, as Scripture teaches, like a mirror (James 1:23-25). One of the most discouraging things I do every day is get up and look in the mirror. I think, "What can I do with this face?" The Bible says the Word of God is like a spiritual mirror. I read it, and I see myself as I really am. And each time my response should be, "What can I do with this?"

James says that since God's Word is like a mirror, pity the man who turns away from the mirror and forgets what kind of man he is. Wouldn't it be terrible if you looked in the mirror in the morning and said, "Well, that's interesting. It doesn't look too good, but thank you for the reflection. See you later"? Mirrors are intended to help us see ourselves for what we really are and, it is to be hoped, to encourage us toward constructive change.

According to Hebrews 4:12, the Word is sharper than a two-edged sword, piercing our being to the marrow. I don't always know why I do the things I do, but the Word of God explains my actions. It is a sharp, two-edged sword that lays me out in divine surgery and says, "Stowell, look at why you did that. You are selfish."

As I was studying the life of Saul recently, I noticed that one of Saul's tragic flaws was that of self-promotion. After one of the battles in which he had compromised the will of God, he was on his way to see the prophet Samuel to tell him what had happened. But he stopped with his men in a particular place and said, "See here, wouldn't this be a good place to build a monument?" (1 Samuel 15:12). The monument, of course, was to Saul himself and to his mighty military victory.

Somewhat self-righteously I thought, *Isn't that interesting? I know a lot of people who build monuments to themselves.* Then the Holy Spirit brought to mind my own fallenness. "What do you mean you know a lot of people who do that? Maybe it's *your* problem, Stowell."

Not too long after that, I was with a friend who had just returned from speaking at a national conference in Canada. He reveled in how thrilling the experience had been. He told me what a tremendous time he had had and how receptive the people had been to the Word of God. But throughout the conversation what did I do? Did I encourage him? Listen carefully and show genuine interest in his happiness? Ask what God did? No. I just looked for a crack in the conversation, so I could say, "Yes, I know, I spoke there last year." And as soon as I had a chance, I did just that.

Immediately, like a two-edged sword, God's Word cut through to my attitude, and His Spirit said, "Stowell, why do you build monuments to yourself?" It was time to change the way I thought, to change my operational conclusions, and to change the way I acted. Like a two-edged sword, the wonder of His Word has worked again.

The Word of God is the wonder of a *seed* that lodges in the soil of the heart and in time takes root and bears the fruit of righteousness (Luke 8:15). It is the wonder of *bread* to the spirit that we may be nourished and strengthened (Deuteronomy 8:3; Matthew 4:4). And it is the wonder of a *house* so strong in its foundations that even great floods cannot move it (Matthew 7:24-27).

In short, the wonder of this Book takes us back to where we started. We desperately need to change the way we think—our operational conclusions and our decisions. The only resource that can effect those kinds of changes is God's Word.

There is no hope for effectively challenging the darkness in our day unless we have a personal, unflinching allegiance to the worth, work, and wonder of the Word of God. That will demand that we be in it often, that our lives be lived under it always, and that we claim it as our sole authority and resource as we make our way through the deepening darkness. With the psalmist we must claim, "Thy Word is a lamp unto my feet and a light unto my path" (Psalm 119:105).

When the Word of God has worked its work in our perceptions, our whole view of life will have changed. We will begin to realize personally what it means that "He delivered us from the domain of darkness, and transferred us to the kingdom of His beloved Son" (Colossians 1:13). We will be transformed in key areas of existence. Money, power, pleasure, relationships, purpose, pain, and other key elements in our lives will be dramatically redefined, and we will be transformed by the renewing of our minds.

5

LIVING ON PURPOSE

Three Essentials for Lighting the Night

As we seek to build a foundation for right thinking and biblically sound life decisions that will penetrate the darkness, the most essential questions we must answer are questions of personal *purpose* in life: Why am I here? For what reason has God put me on earth? How should I think biblically about my purpose in life?

Although at first glance these questions seem philosophical and not nearly as important as our passions for success, happiness, and prosperity, in reality they are the most significant questions we can ask if we are committed to biblical thinking. These questions strike at the heart of life: What is the ultimate purpose for existence?

Secular input gives us confused answers, none of them reliable and all based on secular values. The fallen world system around us claims career, monetary pleasures, comfort, peace, staying on top, and other superficial satisfactions as its statement of purpose. It is, however, a menu of emptiness and ultimate disappointment. As one friend has philosophized, "No one on his deathbed ever wished he had spent more time at the office."

WHOSE VOICE DO WE HEAR?

Our world provides us with no steady, certain purpose for life. Consequently, our lives lack direction. Like meandering streams we randomly move here and there according to the latest cultural whim. Throughout recent decades of secular thought, those whims have changed, and the Christian community has changed with them. In the sixties, for example, the wealth and affluence of the previous generation was thought to be corrupt and invalid. We were encouraged to deny corporate power and greed and to dedicate ourselves instead to the purpose of personal love, peace, community, and a "freethinking" philosophy of life.

As the women's movement flourished in the seventies and eighties, the preeminent purpose for some women became their careers, and they decided against the value of home and family. Home and traditional family values were no longer accepted answers to the questions, "Who am I?" and, "What am I here for?"

Now, several years later, the secular experiment has aged and even soured, and we are hearing new voices. These voices tell us that perhaps it's better for women to put their families first and their careers second. In spite of whatever encouraging signs we might see, however, the cultural values around us continue to ebb and flow in accordance with popular opinion, not absolute truth.

The ever-changing purpose statements of our secular world are perhaps best characterized by the bumper sticker that reads, "Don't follow me—I'm lost!" What are we to think? What are we to believe? Is there any genuine purpose that is true and firm, anything upon which we can build our lives?

Simply denying the purpose statements of the world around us is not enough. The void must be filled with something real and true. Throughout Scripture, whenever we are commanded to turn away from the false or negative, we are told to turn toward God and His truth instead. There is no putting off without putting on; no fleeing without pursuing. We are not here to take up space until Jesus comes. He has a specific purpose in mind for each of us. Being verbally pious and offering statements such as "My purpose is to serve Jesus" is not enough. It is too easy to "serve Jesus" for the wrong reasons, such as self-satisfaction, power, prestige, or public recognition.

Neither is simple survival an adequate purpose for life. For some of us making it to bed at night, whole and in our right minds, is the only purpose we feel we can legitimately handle. But sooner or later that will leave us with a nagging emptiness and lack of direction—because we were designed for much more.

Biblical purpose is a realistic goal, even for the most confused, fast-paced, and complex lives. In fact, biblical purpose provides an attainable, organizing dynamic that gives meaning to even our most "messed up" moments. We need to realize that our unwillingness to tackle the primary issue of purpose does not mean we will not have some purpose in our lives. The truth is that if we don't actively claim that territory of our lives for God, the world system will define it for us. And the world inevitably will determine a costly and undesirable pattern for our lives, not unlike a racquetball ricocheting to and fro against every wall around us. As one Bible expositor has pointed out, "We do not get to choose whether or not we will be slaves. We only choose to whom or what we are enslaved."

Let's face it: we only get one shot at this thing called life. And in the end, when we glance into the rearview mirror, our *purpose* will have written the story of all that is behind us. For some, the pain of a life of misspent purpose will be hard. On the other hand, those who affirm biblical purposes for their lives will have few regrets.

In the Beginning, God . . .

When God created the human race, He also created a well-ordered universe, and He put into it three primary purposes for our existence:

1. REFLECTING

In Genesis 1:26-27 God makes clear that His *first* purpose in creating us was to demonstrate His qualities and His glory *through* us. "Then God said, 'Let Us make man in Our image, according to Our likeness. . . . ' And God created man in His own image, in the image of God He created him; male and female He created them."

God's first ordered purpose for man was that he be an image-bearer. The invisible God made a visible creation: the heavens, the earth, the animal kingdom. All of His creation, particularly man, was to make visible His glory, that is, His nature and character—the sum total of all He is. The crowning glory of His creation was mankind.

It is obvious that "in His image" cannot mean that we physically look like Him. God has no intrinsic physical properties. Nobody looks like God because God is spirit (John 4:24).

So what does it mean to be created in His image? It means we were created with the potential to reflect some of the same characteristics He possesses. He has personality, will, and emotions. He created us with personality so that His personality could be expressed through us. His emotions are reflected in our emotions as we love what He loves and hate what He hates. His will as seen in our wills enables us to show others how God would live on the earth.

The world knows that God is an awesome, masterful Creator. Psalm 19 tells us that the heavens declare the glory of God, and Romans 1:20 says the world knows of His eternal power and divine attributes through His creation. But the world also knows that God is love, righteousness, mercy, and justice because it sees Him in us. As those around us watch the personality, emotions, and will of God flow from our lives, we give visibility and credibility to the invisible, physically distant God.

That is the essence of being an image-bearer. It is what the Bible calls "glorifying God," and it is part of our biblical purpose for life. It is letting the light of God flow through one's being.

2. RULING

His *second* created purpose is seen in Genesis 1:26, which reads, "And let them rule over the fish of the sea and over the birds of the sky and over the cattle and over all the earth, and over every creeping thing that creeps on the earth."

Whereas our purpose in terms of our relationship to God is to display His glory, our purpose in relationship to our world is to rule over it as stewards, or caretakers, of His creation. This purpose of ruling is particularly important in light of the tendency we have to let the material world rule over us.

We are too quickly seduced by the cosmos, or the world system, as Satan uses it to gain mastery over us. It is significant that in his strategic overthrow of God's created order in the Garden, Satan used a piece of God's creation to seduce Eve. Had she claimed in that moment of temptation that it was her purpose to rule over creation—and over the crafty serpent—perhaps she could have resisted the mastery of the tantalizing fruit over her life. But because Eve permitted her passions to be ruled by the elements of creation, Satan gained control of her and of God's created order. From drugs, to sex, to alcohol, to cars, houses, gold, and gems, the creation still seeks to seduce us into bondage.

Biblical purpose lifts us above the destructive, fallen pattern as we claim our privilege to be the stewards of our environment, not slaves to it.

3. RESPONSIBILITY

Our *third* purpose for living is to respond positively to our responsibility to obey His reign in our lives and in our world. In Genesis 2:16-17 Adam and Eve are called to obedience. "The Lord God commanded the man, saying, 'From any tree of the garden you may eat freely; but from the tree of the knowledge of good and evil you shall not eat, for in the day that you eat from it you shall surely die.'"

We were created to submit to God with a sense of moral responsibility. He established His glory in us, gave us responsibility as stewards of His created order, and made us morally responsible and accountable to Him.

Although we rule over His earth, He reigns over us. We are like governors, or administrators, and He is the King. God's reign over our lives provides the key element of a purposeful existence. It's a matter of humility, worship, honor, gratitude, and loyalty that issues in joyful, unflinching submission to God. Not only do we allow Him complete control, but we strive to bring Him glory as well. How would we know what would bring Him glory if He did not communicate how we reflect His character in His Word? Having read His Word, what response is left but to obey and submit to Him?

God's one command to Adam and Eve was that they avoid the tree of the knowledge of good and evil. That command visibly demonstrated the worth of God in their lives—that He is sovereign even over His highest order of creation and worthy of their allegiance. The only way the world could know anything about the invisible God's worth and right to sovereignly reign was by watching Adam and Eve submit daily to their great Creator's command. And if Adam and Eve had fulfilled their responsibility to be obedient and accountable, their world would not rule them. Rather, they would have ruled their world.

A CORD OF THREE STRANDS

These three biblical purposes are woven together into a singular cord of purpose for the Christian. When God reigns in us, we rule over our world according to His reign, and we inevitably bring glory to His name.

On a recent trip to England, Martie and I were struck by the beauty of the gardens at Hampton Court, the historic home of the great Tudor king Henry VIII. We pondered how lush and spectacular it must have been in his day—and then we realized that the caretaker, under the authority of King Henry, was the one who managed the garden in such a way that it brought great honor and glory to the king. The gardener was the key. His commitment to obediently work the ground entrusted to him according to the king's wishes reflected well on the royal name. The situation of Christians is no different.

As we look at Genesis 3:6, it is shocking to see how quickly and totally God's threefold purpose for living was sabotaged. In one fateful act, mankind's purpose was redefined: "When the woman saw that the tree was good for food, and that it was a delight to the eyes, and that the tree was desirable to make one wise, she took from its fruit and ate; and she gave also to her husband with her, and he ate."

What happened to the purpose of reflecting? Eve's purpose suddenly became to live for that which would display *her* wisdom, that which would promote *her* worth. She was motivated by the desire to promote the creature rather than the Creator (see Romans 1:25). Before the entire universe, God's creation refused to give Him the honor due His name. According to Eve, God no longer "deserved" her allegiance. She chose instead to glorify herself.

And what happened to Eve's responsibility of stewardship? She chose to be ruled by creation when she was seduced by a crafty creature and an alluring tree. She expressed disdain for the reign of God and for a morally responsible and accountable life. She decided to do what *she* wanted rather than what God wanted her to do. The divine purpose had been reordered. With one sinful act, Eve (and Adam, too) submitted to Satan's purpose. The cord of three strands was severed first in her thoughts, then in her operational conclusions, and then in her actions.

PURPOSE IN PERSPECTIVE

When boiled down to basics, there are only two patterns of purpose. There is, of course, the fallen purpose of self-glorification, self-gratification with the world around us, and self-determination. Or there is the biblical purpose of showing off the wonder, worth, and qualities of God when we as image-bearers accept His absolute reign in our lives and ourselves as caretakers over the world in which He has placed us.

Life is directed by those three fundamental issues, regardless of the situations that surround us. These are the issues that will transform our thinking. They then become the values that form for us new operational conclusions, which in turn will result in decisions that will begin to ignite rays of light to penetrate our world.

How, then, is this purpose lived out as light in the darkness?

First, if my purpose in life is to reflect His nature and character, then in each situation of life I need to ask myself, *What would be the most accurate reflection of who God is and what He is like?* That will cause me to evaluate all facts and experience not in the light of what benefits me most but in the light of what best reflects the nature and character of God.

That will affect the way I think, the way I speak, and the things I do. As Paul exhorted, "Whatever you do in word or deed, do all in the name of the Lord Jesus, giving thanks through Him to God the Father" (Colossians 3:17). As I reflect on God's forgiveness, love, mercy, grace, patience, purity, integrity, faithfulness, justice, righteousness, willingness to sacrifice, and servanthood, I will give priority to the value of His glory through me and will live out decisions that indeed demonstrate what God is like.

Second, I need to ask myself, *Am I ruling over the creation around me as God intends, or is the world ruling over me?* Romans 12:1-2 admonishes, "I urge you therefore, brethren, by the mercies of God, to present your bodies a living and holy sacrifice, acceptable to God, which is your spiritual service of worship. And do not be conformed to this world, but be transformed by the renewing of your mind, that

you may prove what the will of God is, that which is good and acceptable and perfect.''

Likewise, we are instructed in 1 John 2:15-17, "Do not love the
world, nor the things in the world. If anyone loves the world, the love
of the Father is not in him. For all that is in the world, the lust of the
flesh and the lust of the eyes and the boastful pride of life, is not from
the Father, but is from the world. And the world is passing away, and
also its lusts; but the one who does the will of God abides forever.''

When we choose to *not* let the world rule over us but to rule over
the world by making decisions based on the "good and acceptable and
perfect" will of God, we will not be conformed to this world. Rather,
we will be transformed by the renewing of our minds, which will in
turn lead ultimately to godly decisions.

The extent to which this transformation has taken place will
make itself evident in the ordinary decisions of life. Can we say no to
buying a new car if buying a car would violate clear priorities regarding money, family, or integrity? Are we in control of our thought-life
in regard to the created beauty and power of women or men around
us? Would we violate truth, faithfulness, decency, or obedience to
gain any alluring substance from the creation around us? How we answer those questions reflects the extent to which we have chosen to be
seduced by creation or to be stewards over creation. Third, if God is
to reign in any given situation, I need to ask myself, *What does He
want* me *to do in my created environment in order to glorify Him? How
can I best display His sovereignty, His rule over my life?* These questions
hit at the heart of who is in control of my thoughts, words, and actions. It is one thing to say, "Christ is in control of my life." It is quite
another to prove it through my thought-life, conversations, and life
decisions.

This is where the admonitions of Scripture are either incorporat-
ed into our daily lives in committed submission or ignored. Whether
it is the command for wives to submit to their husbands, or for husbands to love their wives, or for children to obey their parents, we
either submit to God's sovereign authority by obeying His Word, or
we ignore it. We either let Him reign, or we seek to maintain control
of a ship that will soon be careening through relationships and other
significant entities in our existence.

The Deceptive Alternative

There is, of course, an alternate system of purpose. That system is the fallen pattern by which we discount the glory and reign of God and live for the purpose of using creation for our own glory through self-indulgence and self-determination. The ultimate consequence of this system is a life without God's glory or reign, one that grows increasingly entangled in a web of the addictive commodities of our world.

Under this plan, the adversary uses created things to control man for his purposes, playing on our desires for self-glorification, self-indulgence, and self-determination. Satan thus controls our purpose, manipulates our operational conclusions, and revels in swallowing us up in the darkness of our self-defeating and ungodly decisions.

Three issues drive this destructive pattern of purpose.

First, we ask ourselves, *How can I best enhance and advance myself in this situation?* When this is our attitude, even charitable and religious activities can be misused, as can lesser and more obvious expressions of self-advancement. We should never think that those involved in Christian service, such as church, Christian education, or missions, are exempt from this insidious self-glorification. No one is exempt. The only safeguard against it, in fact, is the saturation of one's mind with the biblical purpose for life: to glorify God.

Second, we ask ourselves, *What can I use around me to indulge and gratify myself?* In this issue the rule is "anything goes." As we saw in chapter 3, this is the essence of hedonism, the belief that anything that looks good, feels good, or sounds good *is* good. How unfortunate that we have fallen for the world's indoctrination concerning what we "need" to have a full life. Often it seems that if we can tell ourselves, "I deserve this," we regard an indulgence as fair game. As a result, we have put ourselves back in the position of being ruled by created things that are often addictive rather than our ruling over creation as God planned.

Third, we ask ourselves, *What do I want to do?* Or, *What would please me most?* This is a matter of our ruling our own lives. We throw off the sovereign rule of God and seek what we crave, covet, or "deserve." We believe that in "this particular situation" we know what is really best. When it comes to obeying the Word of God, we obey only when it is convenient or when we can see a personal advantage in doing so. We glibly disobey when obedience does not suit our purpose or offer tangible rewards.

THINKING IT THROUGH

Being committed to God's specific purposes in life would be little more than academic exercise if it didn't produce dramatic results. Under God's ordained purpose, there was peace, harmony, productivity, worth, dignity, freedom, and the promise of a great future. In contrast, the consequence of sinful purposes has been devastation in relationships, lives, homes, business, personal worth, and fulfillment. Either positively or negatively, purpose always produces results. There is always an outcome of one's purpose in life, either for good or for ill. No one escapes this pressing reality.

Of all that the redemptive work of Christ has accomplished, restoration of purpose is perhaps the most significant. This is confirmed repeatedly in the New Testament. First Corinthians 6:20 tells us, "For you have been bought with a price: therefore glorify God in your body." And in Romans 8:29 we read that reflecting is the ultimate goal of our being: "For whom He foreknew, He also predestined to become conformed to the image of His Son."

In short, through His indwelling Spirit our capacity to allow His will, personality, and emotions to flow through us has been restored through Christ's redemptive work. Submission to His reign and godly stewardship of those things with which Satan would otherwise trip us up are the natural expressions of our newness in Christ (Romans 12:2). It is what Paul meant when he wrote, "Therefore if any man is in Christ, he is a new creature: old things are passed away; behold, all things are become new" (2 Corinthians 5:17; KJV*).

Reaching biblical operational conclusions about purpose is clearly one of life's pivotal landmarks. The facts we process daily about family, friends, enemies, cars, houses, careers, time, talents, thoughts, and conversations are constantly with us. What values will translate this deluge of data into godly purposes that will in turn produce significant and satisfying results? The values of God's glory through me by my ruling my personal world under the authority of God.

*King James Version.

WHAT DIFFERENCE DOES IT MAKE?

How does biblical purpose look in shoe leather? What external actions reveal an internal purpose consistent with the nature and character of God? Let's look at a few examples.

Undoubtedly, one of life's most difficult tasks is dealing with those who have hurt, used, abused, or manipulated us. Our purpose in life will determine our response to these trials. Will we take revenge or force separation? Will we resort to slander or self-protection?

If we value the divine purpose, we will determine to obey God and not be ruled by the one who hurt us. We will manage the relationship according to the reigning authority of God, and forgiveness and constructive steps to healing will become our operational conclusions. Self-glorification, self-gratification, and self-determination will be rejected as we begin the difficult but rewarding process of turning our enemy over to God (Romans 12:17-21). We will learn to accept the pain in terms of the constructive growth it will accomplish in us (James 1:1-5), and we will strive to apply forgiveness and unconditional love, regardless of the response of the one who has harmed us.

In the escalating sensuality of our culture, women and men are paraded as objects of sexual satisfaction. Does Satan lure us with these created commodities? Pornography, adulterous affairs, lust, sexual fantasies, impure thought-lives, and all the unsavory rest of it will have no power over those who process the information around them through the threefold purpose of Scripture—reflecting God's image, ruling the created world around us, and responsibility to obey God's reign over us. In our operational conclusions we will value the worth of others, and we will seek to love others purely and to please God by rejecting the seductive draw of our own passions.

What about lying in order to gain advantage? Cheating to stay ahead or get rich or get promoted? Living for the accumulation of created things? All of these ambushes are conquerable only if we have clearly thought through our biblical purpose in life and claimed our minds for God. When we are tempted, we merely say, "Sorry, but that's not what I'm here for," and continue striving for His purpose to be realized in our lives.

Biblical purpose requires that as His image is reflected in us we clearly and tactfully give Him the credit, since all that we are and do is ultimately attributable to Him. Our ability to create is a gift from the creative God. Our intelligence, skills, and accomplishments are all built upon the fact that He has made us like Himself, and He deserves all the credit. As the great composer Franz Joseph Haydn once cried out in his waning years when the audience at a performance of his work broke out in applause directed toward him: "No, No! Not from me, but from thence," he said, pointing upward. "From heaven above comes all!"

Glorifying God through correct conclusions and godly life decisions will reflect the development of His character within us. Qualities such as forgiveness, mercy, compassion, justice, long-suffering, righteousness, and love are clear, visible statements of who God is and what He is like. The purpose of our existence is to showcase the God of the universe through our lives, to make the invisible God visible, to display through our lives the incredible God as entirely credible.

Living out the purpose of God for our lives will set the night ablaze.

6

THE PURSUIT OF HAPPINESS

Lighting the Night with Biblical Fulfillment

If a genie suddenly appeared and offered the choice of either wealth, beauty, fitness, success, popularity, self-fulfillment, or happiness, my guess is that most of us would choose to be happy. Something down inside all of us longs for happiness.

It will come as a surprise to some that God wants us to be happy. He created us to know joy and fulfillment in life. That's why humans —even those outside the kingdom of God—search for happiness. God has created a happiness-shaped void within us. The reason we find it such an elusive dream is that only He can fill that void.

It is just this void that the master of the domain of darkness capitalizes on to misdirect well-intentioned lives. The darkness wrongly concludes that happiness consists of gaining commodities like wealth, beauty, exotic pleasures, security, peace, and acceptance. Happiness, to the fallen system, is found in being free to do all that we want to do. Yet those who drone on in the dark in search of this settled, long-lasting happiness find that although laughter, momentary joy, and an occasional thrill are theirs, happiness as an ongoing quality of life is nonexistent. Apart from God's design, there is no authentic happiness.

Given the driving hunger in all of us for happiness, I do not know of a stronger statement for those of us who bear the torch of light than for us to produce obvious, genuine happiness for all to see.

HAPPINESS IS . . .

The Bible says a great deal about happiness. God not only created us to be happy, He has also shown us the way. The Old Testament word closest to our concept of happiness is the word most of our English versions translate "blessed."

Let's take a closer look at the Hebrew word, so that we can understand what God's kind of happiness is. The Hebrew word for "blessed" has several nuances to it, but basically it means *that which is straight* or *that which is right*. We could say it describes the kind of life that is "right on" or "straight."

Our garage is attached to our house. It's a wonderful convenience in inclement weather, but it's also a terrible temptation because all winter whenever I don't know what to do with something, I put it in the garage. Usually by March I'm so ashamed of my garage I don't want to open it up to the neighborhood.

By contrast, my neighbor's garage faces mine, and he keeps his spotlessly clean. He's one of those people who has a place for everything and keeps everything in its place. He has hangers for his shovel, his hammers, his screwdrivers, and his rakes. He paints his garage floor, and he actually vacuums his driveway. About mid-March it all gets to me, and I finally say, "This Saturday I'm going to tackle the garage." I get up early in the morning, open the door, tear into it, and by 4:00 in the afternoon, I've thrown half of it away. I get all the rest organized. I step back, fold my arms, look around the garage, and feel absolutely fulfilled. In fact, I leave my garage door open for three weeks so that everybody in the neighborhood can see how good it looks!

Biblical happiness is a life without the junk and clutter that a self-oriented life deposits in our spirits. It is a sense of well-being, cleanliness, and organization. It is to live an organized life so that there is the inner sense of well-being that harmony provides. Some of us think of happiness as a twenty-four-hour smile, but that's an awfully shallow definition. What we actually crave is the kind of blessedness that retains a sense of inner peace and joy in spite of adverse circumstances.

That is the kind of blessedness, or happiness, that perseveres even when tears are running down our cheeks and our hearts are broken. It is not a spiritual problem to have a broken heart. Nor is it a spiritual problem when, in the midst of crisis and trauma, tears fill your eyes and stain your face. Jesus wept. He knew about trauma.

But at the bedrock, being happy, or blessed, means we know that everything is all right. That's the kind of biblical happiness God offers us. It is like driving through a speed trap, feeling your blood pressure rise and your heart rate increase as you glance down to see how fast you are going and then noticing that you are right at "55." In that crisis you have confidence that though trouble is lurking in the shadows, your life is straight. You are right on. It's confidence that even when trials claim you for a season you will find true happiness flowing under it all as you claim that God works even all things for good to those who love Him and are called according to His purpose (see Romans 8:28).

Biblical happiness, blessedness, is the deep, settled "all rightness" of your soul.

WHICH FORMULA FOR HAPPINESS?

Understanding our basic hunger for happiness and the essence of true happiness, we need to ask, "How do I get that for my life?" The first chapter of Psalms begins with the word *blessed*. Clearly, this psalm is going to talk about the pursuit of God's kind of happiness and how to receive it. This is a formula psalm, and its "happiness formula" demands a dramatic reordering of our values and conclusions about the pursuit of happiness.

It is interesting that the psalmist begins with a negative. We live in a culture that is decidedly negative about negatives, but it's crucial for us to recognize that any time we are in pursuit of something important, we must eliminate all nonproductive options. The psalmist is saying that we should eliminate the nonproductive, non-happiness options so that we don't waste our time.

Thus verse 1 tells us where this kind of happiness is *not* found. It says, "Happy is the person who walks *not* in the counsel of the wicked" (italics added). That is a reference to the advice the ungodly give us about life and the pursuit of pleasure. The psalm cautions us that if we listen to ungodly input about happiness we will not find it. Regardless of whether we look for happiness in material treasures, horoscopes, soap operas, self-help books, or the *Wall Street Journal*, the counsel of the ungodly will never lead to God's true happiness.

If we see ungodly advice as the daily, cultural input around us, we are right on target. We live in a fallen cosmos. Since the Fall, our world system has been managed, organized, arranged, and driven by the forces of Satan. And at the very center of the cosmos is non-truth. Carried to their logical conclusions, the values and ethics of this world are contradictions of the truth of God. That's why Christ told the Pharisees, "I know that you are of your father the devil, because you lie" (cf. John 8:44). Jesus was saying, "You tell non-truths, and Satan was a liar from the very beginning. We know that his whole system, and everything that pours out of his system, is non-truth." At its core the bulk of the cultural input we receive is untrue, and it is certainly untrue regarding happiness.

SUBTLE SEEPAGE

What is particularly tragic is that many of God's people have bought into the advice of our ungodly culture. It is possible—often probable—that we will receive ungodly advice from a brother or sister in Christ. It is akin to the problem experienced by the church in Corinth, which brought its secular baggage into the kingdom, unpacked it, dressed up in it, and walked around the kingdom of God looking like children of this world.

Ungodly advice does not only come from people "out there"; it has seeped into our pews, pulpits, and publications. What kind of advice has polluted our thought processes, distracted our focus, and diminished our light? What is the culture's ungodly advice about happiness?

WORLD CLASS MISINFORMATION

"ME FIRST"

Our culture tells us that we should live for "number one." We are told that the way to true happiness is to look out for our rights and jealously pursue our privileges. Thinking Christianly immediately casts this advice in the shadow of the truth that living for God and others is what brings ultimate satisfaction. However, the lure of self-centered pursuits to preserve happiness seems to be ever present.

When I was in the pastorate I would occasionally stop by my favorite donut shop on Sunday morning on my way to church, buy a couple of donuts, and take them to my office. I usually got to the shop at about 6:15, which meant that some of the "night people" were still there recovering from Saturday night. One Sunday morning as I stepped up to the counter to order, some guy behind me said, "Two black coffees, please!" I immediately thought, *Wait just a minute! I'm next!* To make it worse, the clerk turned around and started to get him two black coffees.

I started muttering under my breath, and I piously thought, *Well, what can I expect? The guy's a pagan, right? He's bought into the cultural ethic. He's just looking out for number one. Of course!*

That's when the Holy Spirit hit me between the eyes. *Who's looking out for number one, Stowell?* The minister on his way to church, preparing to proclaim the servanthood ethic, was just as concerned about who was first in line!

No believer is exempt from the intrusion of a self-centered, me-first, "look out for number one" attitude. It's the core issue of the flesh, and it's self-promotion. That's the way we are programmed to think, and without the Word of God it will become the value by which we draw all our conclusions and make our decisions.

Some secular studies are now reviewing the sociological phenomena of the "me decade" and its impact on America. In his book *New Rules: Self-fulfillment in a World Turned Upside Down*, Daniel Yankelovich studies what he calls "self-fulfillers." He writes, "The amazing thing . . . was that as we studied the strongest self-fulfillers, we found them to be the least happy people."

It's true. Actualize self-fulfillment, and before long you'll be climbing on people and manipulating them. You will end up in a lonely cavern of life with broken relationships and perhaps a broken heart.

Actor James Cagney died at the age of eighty-six. Though I was never an ardent fan of Cagney, I was impressed by the newspaper article about his death. Before he died, Cagney said, "The greatest joy of my life has been my wife." They had been married for sixty-four years (rare news coming from Hollywood). When somebody asked him why he had been so happy, Cagney replied, "The key to happiness is a total absorption in everything but self."

When the world tells you, "Stick up for number one," don't forget that is the road to brokenness and aloneness, not to happiness.

BEAUTY

What about beauty? It is often trumpeted as a primary source of happiness. Many of us think, *If I were just more attractive, I'd be happy*. We buy brand-name cosmetics and designer clothes. We get face-lifts and mud packs. We buy into the lie that external beauty in and of itself will make us happy and that beautiful people are happy people. But let's not forget Marilyn Monroe, the epitome of beauty in her generation, who took her own life with an overdose of sleeping pills. Or the anonymous thousands like her who crave temporal beauty only to find that life still turns ugly within them and around them.

The Bible is accurate when it tells us, "Beauty is vain" (Proverbs 31:30). Beauty is empty in and of itself; it can do no more than complement—or contrast—what's inside the container.

FITNESS

Our fad-conscious culture is persuaded that "if my body were more fit, more sculpted, I'd be happy. I could just look into the mirror and be happy with myself. I'd feel young again, rejuvenated." Based on that myth, health spas are bulging with men and women who pump iron and exercise in front of the ever-present wall of mirrors.

Much of this preoccupation with fitness stems from our basic fear of the demise of our bodies. We want to stay young and fit. We don't want to feel our bodies sag and grow weak. Although there's nothing wrong with general health and fitness, we simply cannot stay the hand of the aging process. The wrinkles will eventually come, and old age will creep upon us, whether we like it or not.

Even the Bible says it is good to be fit. We need to be good stewards of our bodies. But we must not kid ourselves into thinking that if we could only be disciplined, exercise a lot, and get the body fit again, we would be happy. It's just not true.

WEALTH

Our culture counsels us, "If you had enough money, you'd be happy." That thought permeates our advertisements. "Rich people are happy people," we are told verbally and visually. We drive by a beautiful marina and see all the gorgeous sailboats. We drive through a nice neighborhood and covet the mansions. But the happiness that wealth brings—as we see almost daily in the tragic lives of many—is short-lived and vulnerable.

Remember Howard Hughes, the wealthiest man in the history of America? By the time he died, Hughes was arguably one of the most miserable individuals on earth. He died wealthy—but had become a paranoid recluse, covered with bedsores and surrounded by filth. The next time you drive the streets of a wealthy neighborhood, remember that money does not exempt the rich from broken relationships and loneliness. Wealth is not a ticket to happiness.

Many of us know this, yet we reason, "I don't want that much money. I just want enough to buy a few more things—a small boat, a better car, a ride-on mower, a better vacation. Just a little more will bring fulfillment."

When our children were younger, around Thanksgiving each year they would serve notice with Christmas lists. And, being the "loving" parents we were, we would buy the gifts, wrap them up, and the night before Christmas we'd stack them so high we could barely see the Christmas tree. At 4:30 on Christmas morning, the kids would crash into our bedroom, grab us by the wrists, flip us onto the couch, and dig into the loot—American style.

One year, however, after the traditional glut of gifts, I felt a tug on my pant leg. When I looked down, there were two little eyes looking up at me forlornly. "Yes?" I said.

"Daddy," said my little boy, "I don't have anything to do."

What? I thought. *All my hard-earned money spent on gifts, and he doesn't have anything to do?* I was depressed. But as I thought about it seriously, I realized that it was a perfect illustration of the emptiness and futility of the accumulation of things.

There's a saying that states, "The only difference between men and boys is the price of their toys." We are all like little children who cannot be satisfied by any amount of material goods. Yet we continue to crawl across the desert of life from one material mirage to another. Can there be any doubt that material things, too, are a false hope for happiness?

THE BLESSEDNESS OF THE LAW

Now that we know where we won't find happiness, let us determine how we can get our bearings. What are correct operational conclusions about happiness? What is the biblical way to think about happiness?

In Psalm 1:2 we find an answer. The psalmist writes, "But his [the happy man's] delight is in the law of the Lord." Think about that for a moment: God's rules are the key to our happiness. Unfortunately, a lot of people in our generation never get that straight because, from their perspective, God's rules are like divine handcuffs. They see God's Word as a heavenly straitjacket, as though every time something seems fun or enjoyable, God is saying, "You can't do that." And they think that when something seems difficult, God seems to be saying, "That's what I want you to do."

Are God's rules in place to keep us sober and serious, to cut the fun out of our existence? No, indeed. If we think they are, we've bought into the lie of the darkness, of the one who seeks to destroy our minds and lives.

How does God's law directly lead to our happiness? How does the "blessed" person delight in God's Word instead of absorbing the world's programming? To understand the role of God's Word in our thinking about happiness, we need to note several things.

First, the law of the Lord originates in God Himself, and God cannot contradict Himself. He could not possibly give us a set of laws that would be damaging, wicked, unkind, unloving, imperfect, or unrighteous. Remember that as the Israelites began their wilderness trek, God in essence told them not to forsake His law because He had given it to them that they might prosper (see Joshua 1:8).

The goodness of God's law is not just an Old Testament concept. Throughout the book of 1 John we are reminded that the key to loving God is obeying His commands: "For this is the love of God, that we keep His commandments; and His commandments are not burdensome" (5:3). They only become a burden when we make them such.

God's rules are intended to guarantee our success. One evening after supper my then five-year-old son, Joe, came up to me with his bat over his shoulder, his glove in his hand, and his baseball hat on his head a little crooked. "Dad," he said, "I'm going out to play ball."

"Great," I said. "Where are you going to play?"

You can guess where the best place was in the neighborhood to play ball—out in the street. That's where all the older boys played ball, and that's where Joe thought he needed to play in order to be happy.

I put my arm around his little shoulders, pulled him close, and said, "Joe, you may not understand what I'm going to say, but I love you. I want you to enjoy baseball and live a long, happy life. Because of that, I can't let you play ball in the street. I want you to play ball— you can play in the park, or you can play in the backyard. But you can't play in the street because there is danger out there. Quite frankly, I don't want your little body smashed into the grillwork of a Mack truck." That is the essence of the relationship between God's love for us and His commands. We need to remember that God knows much more about Satan's "traffic" than we do. We are inept spiritually to perceive all the danger around us. So in a wonderful act of love, God gave us a Book to tell us about the traffic and to keep us out of it.

When it's hard to obey God, we need to remember that His commands are an expression of His love. As such, Psalm 1:2 states them as the key to a blessed, happy life.

DRUDGERY OR DELIGHT?

The text of Psalm 1 clearly qualifies what the law of God means to the blessed man: "His *delight* is in the law of the Lord." What does it mean to delight in something? This Hebrew word is extremely graphic; it literally explodes with meaning. It means to be absolutely, emotionally and mentally, preoccupied with something.

If you have a teenage daughter or know one, you have probably seen some of what it means to be emotionally and mentally preoccupied. Imagine a teenage girl who, for the past six months, has been watching a guy named Jim. At school she schedules her passing between classes so that she is right where Jim is as he moves from class to class. But, alas, Jim pays no attention to her.

One day, however, the phone rings. She answers it and gasps. "Oh, Jim, hi!" From that moment on, everything in life is Jim. The next morning her nine o'clock class offers the best teacher she's ever had. Normally, she sits on the front row taking copious notes. But not this Wednesday morning. Today she finds any open seat, lands in it, and doesn't hear a word that's said. Instead she draws hearts all over her book, writes "Me + Jim," and draws arrows through the hearts with blood drops coming down.

She has a great youth pastor, and on Wednesday nights she goes to youth group. Normally she loves it but not tonight. She has other things on her mind. In fact, do you know what she's done? She has begun to delight in *Jim*. He has become an emotional, mental preoccupation that totally rearranges her life. Since Jim called, this girl's life is different. She can't get him out of her mind. *That* is what it means to delight in the law of the Lord.

Believing that God has loved us so much that He gave us rules to protect us from Satan's schemes and to guide us into true happiness, we should let His Word preoccupy our thoughts, rule the way we process information, mandate our operational conclusions, and direct our decisions—especially where that elusive goal of "happiness" is concerned. In short, delighting in His law is a strategic step toward a happy life.

The text goes on to say that our delight in God's Word should lead to our *meditating* on it as well. The psalmist wrote, "His delight is in the law of the Lord, and in His law he meditates day and night."

The amazing thing about this formula is that nowhere in this psalm does the psalmist ever say to *do* the law of God. If I had written this psalm, I probably would have said, "You won't find happiness in the advice of an ungodly culture, but get busy and obey God. Just do it!"

The psalmist, however, never says that. Why not? Because if we delight in God's law and meditate on it, we will automatically live in the center of His wonderful will.

God has laws, rules, patterns, and principles that govern the full spectrum of our lives—from our thought-lives to our money, to our families, to our relationships, to the immoral culture around us, to our friends, to our businesses, to our material possessions, to our physical bodies, to our hearts. As these designs organize our thinking and living, we will be led to productive aand ultimately happy lives. In every issue of life, God has clear direction for us, that we might order life well and that, at the core, we might sense that our lives are straight, safe, secure, and blessed in Him. God's directives keep the junk and clutter of sin out of our lives.

LUSH GROWTH AND FRUITFULNESS

We can't ignore the metaphor in verse 3. Anyone who delights in the law of God is like a tree planted by the place where two rivers intersect, with water nourishing it from both sides. When we are firmly planted in the law of God, we can draw all our sustenance from following God's recommendations. Only in this way can we process the information around us according to real truth, not the false truth of our culture. We can form valid operational conclusions and make life decisions that result in true, inward, biblical happiness.

We will be fruitful as well. Our "leaf does not wither" because we are drawing our sustenance from the Word of God. It's not that we don't feel the heat of pressure; it's that when the pressure is on, we don't wither under the crisis. Our sustenance does not come from the environment around us; it lies in the resources of God's Word. No matter how hot, dry, and parched it gets "out there," our leaves will remain strong, and everything we do will prosper—but only when our lives are firmly planted in the law of God. Blessed is the person who falls in love with the law of God, who delights and meditates in it and orders his life by it. Deep within him he has a clean conscience and a wonderful sense of rightness. That is the key to happiness.

When I was in seminary, I had a preaching engagement in Cleveland, and after the service a doctor asked me if I'd come to his home and meet a friend of his. Martie and I followed the map he had given us and drove into a beautiful neighborhood, down a wooded driveway, and up to a large house.

When we went inside, the doctor introduced me to a fellow named Bob. During the course of the evening Bob said to me, "Joe, let me tell you what God has done in my life.

"When I was a boy," he began, "my dad was very successful. But he used to always say to me, 'Bob, you're going to be nothing but a bum.' I hated my father and couldn't wait to get out of the house. When I finished high school, I went to the University of Miami just to get away from home.

"After one quarter at Miami, I dropped out and started wandering the beaches—wine, women, drugs, the whole bit. I thought I was having a ball, but my life started to slowly unravel. Then one day I was on the beach alone, and I looked at myself and realized that what my dad had said was coming true. I was nothing but a bum.

"It made me so mad I stood up and resolved I'd make something out of my life. I was going to prove my dad wrong." And he did. He moved back to Ohio and opened a business that was creative and successful. The night that we met him he wasn't even thirty years old, but it was his Lincoln Continental parked out front.

He said, "Joe, I have everything I could want—a house in the country with horses and fences. I'm married to a beautiful woman. Yet I realized that inside I wasn't happy. I had tried it all from life on the beach to the top of the business world. But the emptiness was so profound that I considered suicide on three different occasions."

Then one night his wife, Mary, came home and said, "Bob, I've found the answer in Jesus Christ." The doctor's wife had led her to the Lord. That bothered Bob greatly. He said, "You've got to be kidding! Religion is for the blind and lame. We don't need that. We've got everything we need!" He put phenomenal pressure on her, but the more pressure he put on her, the stronger and more beautiful she became.

"Finally," he said, "one day I was all by myself in Dayton, Ohio, and I knelt down next to my bed. I lifted my eyes and said, 'God, if you want me, as miserable as I am, here I am. I want You to come in and give me what my wife has. I would like to receive Your Son as my Savior.'"

Since that time, he said, the doctor and his wife had been discipling them. "For months we've been learning a new way to live." He paused, and then his face broke into a smile. He said, "You know, Joe, since we've learned how to live according to God's Word, we've never been so happy."

They had discovered the secret of Psalm 1. As C. S. Lewis wrote, "God cannot give us happiness and peace apart from Himself, because it is not there. There is no such thing."

7

TRIUMPH IN TROUBLE

Responding When Life Is Uncomfortable

Not long ago, Martie and I decided to take one of those days we rarely seem to have time for anymore. It was shortly after Christmas, and our two oldest children had left for a trip with college friends. Our youngest child, Matthew, was still at home, but he and two other friends had been looking forward all vacation to this particular Saturday. They were going to drive three hours north to Wisconsin to go skiing.

Martie and I were delighted about the prospect of having an entire Saturday to ourselves. We would get up leisurely, make coffee, and sit and chat. In the evening we were going to sit by the roaring fire as the snow fell outside, put up our feet, read, and relax all by ourselves. It sounded delightful.

On Friday Matthew came to me and said, "Dad, we want to leave early in the morning—at seven. So would it be OK if my two friends stayed overnight?"

I said, "No problem."

However, he didn't tell me that his two friends had obligations Friday night. They came dragging in at 12:15 A.M. while we waited up to make sure everybody got in.

Then Matthew announced that he couldn't find his wallet. His two friends were not of driving age yet, so Matthew was supposed to do the driving the next day. We had to find that wallet. We looked all over the house, and he even drove back to a friend's house at 1:30 A.M. But we could not find Matthew's driver's license. So I wrote a nice note for him to take: "To whom it may concern: This boy is my son, Matthew. He has my permission . . . just last night he lost his wallet . . .," and so on. He also had a certificate from his temporary license to take with him. At last we got everybody packed up, and we went to sleep. Little did I know what the next day would hold.

The next morning I woke up and looked outside. My driveway was a sheet of ice. I went down to the kitchen and said, "Boys, did you look outside yet?"

"Yes." They looked at me with forlorn expressions as if to say, "You wouldn't tell us we can't go skiing after we waited all vacation for this day, would you?"

I'm a pushover, I admit. I said, "I'll tell you what I'll do. Just to be safe, let me drive out onto the main roads to see whether or not everything is OK." So I jumped into my car in my bathrobe, skidded down the driveway, and got onto the main streets. They were clear as a bell; everybody was moving at regulation speed. So about a quarter-mile down the street I started to turn around. I slowed down and then turned into a parking area—without noticing that it was sheer ice. My car started sliding, and my front right wheel hit the curb with all the weight of my car against it. It made a horrible noise. The only way I could keep the car going straight as I struggled home was to turn the steering wheel all the way in one direction. Somehow, I got the car to wobble into our driveway. Unfortunately, this was the car the boys had planned to take.

I walked inside and told the boys, "You're not going to believe this. I just wrecked my car." We had a second car, a Volkswagen Rabbit® that was rather old and beat-up but relatively reliable. "We only have one option left," I said. "If you guys want to go, you'll have to take the Rabbit." They groused about it, but finally they got everything inside the Rabbit, and off they went.

Finally, Martie and I were alone, though we were still a little concerned about whether the boys would make the trip safely. Halfway there, Matt called: "Dad, we made it this far, and everything's fine."

I said, "Fine. An answer to prayer, Matthew. Keep driving safely." About another hour and a half went by, and I got another telephone call.

Matt said, "Dad, we're here."

"Oh, good. I guess everything went fine."

"Well, not exactly. About a mile and a half from the ski resort the windshield wipers started slowing down, the radio stopped working, the lights started to dim, and finally they went out. Then the car quit. Some guy came along in a pickup truck and towed us up to the parking lot. What should I do?"

"Ask if there is a decent mechanic around. See if you can get his phone number, and I'll call him." So I called the mechanic, who said he'd look at the car, tow it back to the garage, and see if he could fix it. Two hours later, the mechanic called back to say the alternator had burned out and that he couldn't get a new one until Tuesday. After several unsuccessful attempts, we finally made contact with Matt and told him the car wouldn't be fixed until Tuesday. He said, "No problem, Dad. We found some friends who are here with their parents. They're staying in a motel about fifteen miles away, and their parents said we could stay in the room with them."

Later that night we got yet another telephone call from Matt. "We're here, Dad. In fact, when we checked in they had extra rooms, so I just got us our own room." I had given Matt my credit card "in case of emergency," so now this innocent little skiing trip was beginning to register phenomenal dollar signs in my mind.

I said, "OK, Matt, fine. I'll pick you guys up tomorrow morning." The next day I drove seven hours round trip and brought the boys safely home. End of story, right? Not quite.

The car was going to be ready Tuesday night. So Martie and I decided that Wednesday night after work we'd drive up to Wisconsin to pick up the car. As we were driving, however, I began to get tired, so I said, "Martie, would you drive for a while?"

"No problem," she said. I pulled onto the shoulder of the interstate and opened the door—and just as I did, an eighteen-wheeler went screaming by. The wind shear caught the door and ripped it out of my hands. When I tried to shut it, I discovered that the door had been sprung. Need I say more?

THE TRUTH ABOUT TROUBLE

I have a friend who says that the trouble with life is that it is "so daily." No matter who you are or where you are, trouble is inevitable. In Job we read that "man is born for trouble, as sparks fly upward" (Job 5:7). Not one of us is exempt.

Given that fact, we need to discover the truth about trouble. Our world likes to tell us that trouble is *always* unwelcome. In fact, we are told to do everything possible to avoid problems, pain, or crises that might come into our lives. The darkness we live in is more than willing to break up a home just because it is "troublesome" when life is not comfortable anymore. When the thought of children is "troublesome," we simply abort them. Francis Schaeffer was right when he observed that "the two things that Americans are into today are affluence and personal peace—personal peace meaning a life that is devoid of pain and trouble and grief."

But is that the way Christians should think? Admittedly, even Christians have been programmed to process trouble in terms of the priority of personal comfort at all cost. But if we are truly going to be set apart as unique lights in the ever-increasing darkness, we need to let God's wonderful, working, worthwhile Word change the way we think about and respond to trouble.

What, then, is the truth that can set us apart and make us different as we experience life's inevitable troubles? What is the truth about trouble?

The truth from God is that when trials come to us, they are used by God to make us, not break us. They are used to refine us, mold us, mature us, and conform us to the image of God's Son. That's God's truth about trouble.

James 1 outlines the process that leads to productive operational conclusions about crises and pain. We will see that again we have the opportunity to choose God's thoughts over the world's programming and make life decisions based on His conclusions, not our own.

WELCOME TROUBLE?

The book of James begins, "James, a bond-servant of God and of the Lord Jesus Christ, to the twelve tribes who are dispersed abroad, greetings. Consider it all *joy*, my brethren, when you encounter various trials, knowing that the testing of your faith produces endurance. And let endurance have its perfect result, that you may be perfect and complete, lacking in nothing" (vv. 1-4, italics added). The Phillips translation renders it, "My friends, when trouble enters your life, do not resist it as an enemy, but welcome it as a friend." Immediately it is clear that the advice from the Word of God is dramatically different from what our old, fallen natures and worldly culture tell us.

In this passage are several major dynamics that enable us to respond positively to trials, draw radically different conclusions, and practice God's truth about trouble in our daily decisions. Let's look at four major concepts and then focus on five facts that we can count on when trouble comes our way.

The first thing to note is the scope of this perspective on trouble. Earlier I described an innocent kind of episode that managed to turn our lives upside down and shatter our expectations. But there are troubles in life far deeper, more lasting, and more significant than an unexpectedly expensive and chaotic ski trip. There's the trouble of a lost spouse, of a wayward child, of a broken home, or broken health. There's the trouble of severe disappointment with other people, of being plagued by enemies who seemingly want to destroy your reputation and your life. Some of life's troubles are deep, significant, and long lasting, whereas others are not so grave.

What we need to understand from James 1 is that God's truth about trouble applies to us whether our troubles are as simple as a ski trip or as deep and devastating as the death of a loved one. How do we know that? Because the text says, "Consider it all joy, my brethren, when you encounter *various trials*" (italics added). That literally means all kinds of troubles. From the smallest to the largest, from burned up alternators to burned out lives, God's Word tells us how we should think about each and every one.

CONSIDER . . .

Notice that this verse says, "*Consider* it all joy"; it does not say that we should *feel* it a thing of joy when trouble enters our lives. We make a big mistake when we tell one another, "Feel joyful, no matter what. That's what James says." When we say that, we insinuate that true spiritual victory means walking through life with smiles on our faces regardless of the circumstances. We put people under tremendous pressure to be superficial and plastic about life, but we cannot expect them to show up at church beaming, even when their hearts are broken.

James does *not* command us to be any less or more than real people. Remember, even Jesus wept. Christ's heart was broken when He looked at the multitudes of Jerusalem who would not come to Him, and He shed tears when He stood at the tomb of Lazarus.

The word *consider* is borrowed from the accounting profession. It literally means to make a mental note of, to count, to consider, or to reckon on a ledger. It does not deal with how we feel but with how we think and respond. It tells us that when trouble impacts our lives, something needs to be reckoned in our brains. This affects the way we process information, draw conclusions, and make decisions. The one who "considers" is not concerned with changing the circumstances but with changing his or her attitudes and actions in the face of the circumstances.

What is the concept that needs to be "reckoned"? It is the radical thought that when trouble strikes, the circumstance—regardless of what it is—is worth thinking about from a *joyful* perspective. It is to be seen as a thing of joy, and we must honestly consider it that way. It is as though when trouble enters our lives we have numerous columns in which to tally the experience, just as an accountant has numerous columns in his ledger in which to make an entry.

There is, for example, a column called Blame. As trouble hits, we say, "I know what I'll do. I'll blame everyone around me for the problem." So we take our mental pencil and in our mental ledger put a check mark under Blame.

There's another column called Self-pity. Trouble comes along, and we're not violent or militant; we just feel sorry for ourselves. We throw a pity party. Of course, we don't ever invite anybody else to our pity party, because they'd wreck it. They'd try to cheer us up, or tell us it's not so bad. When trouble comes, many of us prefer to consider it unfair affliction.

Still others mark the ledger under the column of Bitterness, or Revenge. It's amazing how creative we can be in our revenge when someone causes us trouble. Since trouble often comes through unpredictable circumstances, we respond bitterly toward God Himself. Whether directed toward people or toward God, the Bitterness-Revenge column is often crowded with check marks.

While at a lunch with two leading Christian counselors, I asked, "What do you think the root problem is for most people who come in for counseling?" Without hesitation, each said that the most significant problem among Christians today is bitterness, either toward other people or toward God. That shouldn't surprise us. Hebrews 12:15 warns us to "see to it that no one comes short of the grace of God; that no root of bitterness springing up causes trouble, and by it many be defiled."

There are numerous other columns in our mental ledger. Some people have a well-used Unfair column, an Escape column, a Withdrawal column, or an Anger column. There are many, many ways we can consider, that is, *think* about, trouble when it enters our lives. But the Bible says that when it comes our way, we need to move all the way across the ledger to the Joy column and put a check there.

We may not *feel* joyful. In fact, that might even be an abnormal feeling for us to have. It might be hard for us to imagine or to understand how a particular episode could ever turn out to be something joyful. Yet the Bible says that mentally we need to *consider* it a thing of joy, knowing that its ultimate end will be positive.

KNOWING . . .

The joy response cannot stand alone. It is possible only in relationship to what you *know*. Shortly after the bitter fighting at Gettysburg, which halted the progress of Lee's mighty army of Northern Virginia into northern territory, Lee wrote to Confederate President Jefferson Davis: "We must expect reverses, even defeats. They are sent to teach us wisdom and prudence, to call forth greater energies, and to prevent our falling into greater disasters." Lee's response to adversity was informed by what he knew of the outcome of adversity. Our response to the setbacks of spiritual warfare should be no less sure.

James refers to this principle: "Consider it all joy, my brethren, when you encounter various trials, *knowing* . . " (italics added). James made clear to his readers that he wasn't talking about some kind of mental reckoning with no substance. It's not an empty promise of blind, shallow, fleeting joy. Rather, there are some things we can *know* for certain that enable us to consider it a thing of joy when trials and troubles come upon us. The Bible encourages us to use our minds to form certain conclusions that will change the way we react.

When we encounter trouble, many of us find that our minds tend to get a little fuzzy and that clear thinking eludes us. Trouble—especially over the long term—tends to confuse us and confound our thinking processes. However, we can delight in the fact that in the midst of trouble there are some things we can always know; and the knowledge of those things enables us to count any trial or trouble a thing of joy.

If a doctor has ever told you that you needed surgery, it's unlikely that you responded by saying, "Oh, Doctor, that's wonderful! When you said that, I felt such a warm glow flow over me. Doctor, I feel so joyful about this! Can we do it right now?" Obviously not. When the doctor said, "Surgery," you probably thought, *This is going to hurt. I don't want any part of this.*

So why did you go through with the pain and trouble of surgery? What did you know ahead of time that enabled you to voluntarily put yourself through that agony? You knew that it would have a good final result. You knew it was something you needed. Perhaps you also knew that the doctor had a good reputation in this area or that someone else had undergone the same surgery with good results.

Regardless, the fact that you knew certain things enabled you to recognize that ultimately the surgery would be good for you. That enabled you to endure the trouble with patience, tranquillity, and perseverance, to "count" it a thing of joy.

The ancient Chinese had a unique mechanism for presenting their plays. They would present a play on a two-level stage. On the upper stage, the resolution of the drama was acted out as the story unfolded below. So as tension and mystery were building on the first level, the audience watching the resolution of the plot would yell to the people on the first level, "Hang in there! Don't give up! If you only knew!" What inspired that hope? It was the knowledge of what was happening on the second level.

I will never forget the 1980 Olympics hockey match between the U.S. team—composed of small, young, amateur players—and the Soviets. During the final period I was literally on the edge of my seat. I felt all the agony and anxiety of the contest as I watched it on television—and then suddenly we scored to go ahead late in the game! *Can we hang on?* I was tense, nervous, and traumatized. Our team went on to win, and I at last was ecstatic.

Later that night the network broadcast a replay of the game, so I invited some friends over to watch it. I watched the same game again, but was I on the edge of my seat? Of course not. I sat back, propped up my feet, had a bowl of popcorn, and leisurely sipped a Pepsi.® I was watching the very same game—but what I *knew* about the outcome made a radical difference in my attitude and actions.

That's exactly what the Bible is telling us in James 1. We will never be able to respond to trouble biblically and to count it a *joy* until we know certain things. What are those things we can know? Let's look at five specific facts we can count on, which we can integrate into our thought processes whenever trials and troubles invade our lives. We can count on these as God's truth. And now is the time to learn them—not after our lives have been shredded by a crisis. It is extremely difficult to learn and implement these facts under the pressure and confusion of trials, so we should learn them while our minds are clear and we can commit them to our long-term memory.

SUPERNATURAL OPTIONS

The first thing we can know for sure is that God has supernatural options with which to help us that we have never dreamed of. Second Peter 2:9 tells us that the Lord knows how to rescue the godly from trials.

I find that many times when trouble comes my way, it's like being in a room with no windows and no doors. I feel like four dark, walls are pressing in against me. To my mind, there are no possible solutions. Yet God knows exactly how He will deliver me.

Think of when the people of Israel were up against the formidable obstacle of the Red Sea. They had been delivered from Egypt by miraculous events but now had their backs to the water, with a horde of Egyptian soldiers bearing down on them. They reasoned, *God brought us out here into the wilderness to kill us. We would rather have been slaves in Egypt that to die out here* (Exodus 14:10-11). But God had options they had never dreamed of. God knew how to deliver His people in time of trouble.

We can know that God already knows how He will deliver us. Even though we can't see them, He has supernatural options, and He will provide a way of escape.

THE TRUTH OF "BEARABILITY"

The second thing we can know for certain is what I like to call the truth of "bearability." First Corinthians 10:13 tells us, "No temptation has overtaken you but such as is common to man; and God is faithful, who will not allow you to be tempted beyond what you are able, but with the temptation will provide the way of escape also, that you may be able to endure [bear] it."

Though we usually think this verse is talking about temptation, its wording in the original language of the New Testament actually applies it to all kinds of trials. God has not given us any trial or trouble that is not common to all people. Furthermore, He will not give us more than we can bear, and with the trial He will provide a way of escape. Remember this: if God permits trouble to come into our lives, we will be able to bear it. He promised He will not give us anything we cannot bear.

As the saying goes, "the God who knows our load limit limits our load." What kind of a Father in heaven would God be if He dumped trials and troubles on us that would crush and defeat us? First Corinthians 10:13 guarantees that all things that come our way will indeed be bearable. That is the truth of bearability.

Our family used to live near a store that gave us credit when we took our pop bottles back. I did not especially like to take pop bottles back to the store, nor did Martie. It was a great marital standoff in the Stowell home! So our garage gradually filled up with pop bottles.

One day I finally thought, *Be a good husband, Stowell. You know you've been a wretch for a whole month now, so just go out there and take the pop bottles back to the store.* As I was leaving, our son Matthew, who was about four, came out and said, "Daddy, can I help you?"

I said, "Sure, Matt," and he picked up a carton of bottles and put them in the car. When I got to the store I said, "Matt, just grab that carton." I picked some up and put them under my arms, and as we started toward the store I watched little Matthew. He wanted so badly to carry his share! But as he shuffled along next to me, all bent over, he got about halfway to the door and said, "Dad, I can't carry this anymore."

Do you suppose I said, "Listen, kid, you started this, so pick that load up right now. You wanted to do this, you asked for it, you deserve it, now you get those bottles into that grocery store"? Of course not. I knew Matt couldn't carry that carton by himself. So I took the load from him. I didn't require him to carry the load anymore because he couldn't bear it. In the same way, the principle of bearability assures us that when trouble comes, the Lord knows what we can bear and will never permit an ounce of extra trouble.

Remember that God stands like a sentinel at the gate of our lives, and nothing moves through the gate without the divine, sovereign permission of God (Job 1). He weighs it all out. He knows us personally and intimately, and He permits nothing that we cannot bear.

SUPPORTING GRACE

Third, we can understand the great truth of God's support. We know from 2 Corinthians 12:9-10 that the apostle Paul struggled with a phenomenal problem he called his "thorn in the flesh." It was so much trouble to him, in fact, that he prayed three times that God would deliver him from it. If anybody had a direct pipeline in prayer, it was Paul. Yet God said no. God made clear to Paul that He had given that trouble to him so that in his weakness he would become strong in the Lord. Paul wrote, "And He has said to me, 'My grace is sufficient for you, for power is perfected in weakness.'" He went on to say that he was content with weaknesses: "For when I am weak, then I am strong." God's supporting grace made the difference for Paul. And God's supporting grace will make the difference for us.

As a pastor for seventeen years, I have stood by people who went through incredible problems and deep pain. And most of the time, I found that they survived amazingly well. I would walk away thinking, *If that were me, I would have been a basket case.* Then I would remember the marvelous truth that when God permits trouble, He gives sufficient grace to supernaturally support us in our pain. According to 1 Peter 5:5 and Hebrews 12:15, the only way we can short-circuit God's grace in a time of trouble is to have a proud spirit or to become bitter. God gives grace. We know it and can count on it.

SUPERNATURAL POWER

Fourth, we can know that God is willing to share His supernatural power with us in the midst of our problems. God supernaturally intervenes.

Some might blindly say, "I've had lots of problems, but I've never seen the power of God in them." If that's the case, perhaps we should think of all the power He has expended to eliminate those things that would have put us over the edge. Some nights, in fact, I go to bed praying, "Lord, I want to thank You for keeping me from those things I didn't even know about, things that would have totally done me in." That protection is the real power of God in my life.

Throughout Scripture, we see that God expends His divine, supernatural power for His people in the midst of problems. God is always the God of the possible. When the Lord reproved Sarah for her unbelief He asked, "Is anything too difficult for the Lord?" (Genesis 18:14). God is always willing to extend His supernatural power in His *perfect timing* for those who are in trouble.

PROCESS WITH A PURPOSE

Finally, when we come face-to-face with trouble, we can know that it is a process with a purpose. "Consider it all joy, my brethren, when you encounter various trials, knowing that the testing of your faith produces endurance. And let endurance have its perfect result, that you may be perfect and complete, lacking in nothing." God is never careless with us, His precious, blood-bought children. Any time He permits trouble and pain, it is always a process with a purpose.

Note what the purpose is: God wants us to be mature. He wants us to grow up to be like Jesus Christ. Biblical maturity is defined for us as coming into the measure of the fullness of Christ (Ephesians 4:13). That demands character, and problems forge character in our lives.

When I am just floating along with few problems, I find that I am much more vulnerable to forgetting how much I need God. I settle back into the groove of my self-sufficiency and think, *Maybe I'm OK just as I am.* On the other hand, troubles reveal what I'm like on the inside. Troubles reveal those things that need to be changed in my life in order for me to mature and to become more conformed to the image of Christ. And my troubles stimulate my devotion to Christ and my dependence on Him.

The *trouble* with trouble is that it exists. It always has, and it always will. "Man is born for trouble, as sparks fly upward" (Job 5:7). That's the trouble with trouble.

The *truth* about trouble is that God is greater. Therefore, we can triumph in trouble. He can cause us to see our troubles as a cause for ultimate joy, not debilitating grief. He gives us the divine perspective so that we might think clearly in the midst of trouble and draw operational conclusions that will produce godly decisions, decisions of forgiveness, patience, and productivity in the midst of pain. He will use trouble to make us more like His Son, Jesus Christ. What greater light could there be than to announce through our trials to a dark and troubled world that troubles don't break us but rather make us! Though we don't look forward to them, when they come we can welcome them as friends.

A doctor tells his patients, "This may hurt you, but I guarantee it will help you." Is that not the assurance of James 1? When our loving Great Physician allows the pain of trials and various troubles to enter our lives, He uses them to help us become "perfect and complete, lacking in nothing."

In a world addicted to comfort, peace, and convenience at any cost, when trouble embitters the human spirit, what a blaze in the night is the life that responds with confidence.

Yet another dynamic in response to trouble is yielding patiently to it. James 1:4 states, *"Let* endurance have its perfect work" (italics added). Patiently yielding is strategic in the process.

Imagine the surgeon striding into the operating room, putting on his gloves, and suddenly noticing that the patient has leaped from the table. He can't effectively work on a moving, resisting target. Relax. Recognize God's goodness and ultimate purpose, and patiently trust His timing.

Resist the urge to take everything into your own hands, to manipulate, to blame, to seek revenge and inflict pain. Remember He seeks to work on you. Yield to His purpose.

Then, pray. "If any of you lacks wisdom, let him ask of God" (James 1:5). As we consider trouble a thing of joy, based on what we know to be true, and as we yield to God's perfecting work, when we don't know what to do, we are to pray. This significant step focuses us away from the temporal pain and onto the character and directives of our eternally good Father. In prayer we are reminded of His goodness, His power, and His plans and principles. In prayer we sense His peace, which passes all understanding (Philippians 4:6).

Prayer puts it all in perspective. Prayer forces us to see our situation from His point of view. Prayer puts us face to face with our God. And as we see his brilliant character and glory, we will say with Job, "Though He slay me, I will hope in Him" (Job 13:15).

8

PUTTING PEOPLE IN THEIR PLACE

Love That Lights the Night

People. They're everywhere. They are the source of our greatest joys and of our greatest frustrations.

We work with them. We live with them. They come in all shapes, sizes, styles, temperaments, colors, and backgrounds. We can't live with them, but we certainly can't live without them. As much as people may frustrate us, the world would be a terribly lonely place without them.

Three men marooned on a desert island found an ancient brass lamp. They rubbed it, and, as you might expect, a genie appeared. The genie granted the men one wish apiece. The first man said, "Boy, I really miss my brokerage in Boston." *Whoosh!* He was gone, back to Boston. The second man pined, "Oh, I miss my family in Cleveland. I wish I could be home with them." *Whoosh!* He was gone like the first. The third looked around and said, "My, it's lonely here. I wish my friends were back!"

Given the ever-present reality of people and their influence in our lives and given the distorted values about people that the darkness promotes, we need to permit Scripture to put people in their place.

THE WORLD'S "TRUTH" ABOUT PEOPLE

In John 17 Jesus Christ prays that believers would not be taken out of the world system but rather that they would be set apart, sanctified, and made unique while they are still in the world. That is only possible through the vehicle of truth—and His Word is truth. As we have already noted, the truth of God is the vehicle that makes us unique, as light in darkness and as salt in a rotting world. God's truth transforms us into effective vessels for Jesus Christ.

What is the truth about people? God's truth about them, we will find, is radically different from what our world tells us and what we often feel inside. We do not need the world to tell us how to respond to people "naturally." We do that on our own.

The world's point of view is that the people around us need to be controlled. If we can control others then they won't hurt us, we won't be vulnerable to them, and they may even live up to our expectations.

Our world system says that people are to be manipulated to serve our own self-indulgent purposes. People are to be climbed on, tolerated, and abused. The essence of the world's view of people is summed up in the question, "What can people do for *me?*"

No one is exempt from this kind of thinking. How many of us, for example, have walked into church thinking, *I wonder if anybody here will say hi to me.* We wonder, *Will anybody encourage me? Will anybody comfort me? Will anybody help me?* That's a classic symptom of the world's perspective on people.

We waltz into relationships with lists of expectations. As a pastor for many years, I had the joy of performing many weddings. I knew that every bride who walked down the aisle and every groom who stood at the front of the church had a long list of expectations. I doubt that many of the couples I married began their relationship saying, "I just can't wait to see what I can do for that other person for the rest of our lives." Instead, he was probably thinking, *I wonder if she'll be a good cook.* She was probably asking herself, *I wonder if he'll be a good father.* He has dreams of what she will do for him. *How will she keep house? Will she keep the children in line, prepare lovely dinners with nice linen tablecloths and candles, clean up after dinner, and put the kids in bed—and then be a tiger in the bedroom?*

She has her dreams, too. Surely after those wonderful dinners, he will help her clear the table and do the dishes. He will be a sensitive, caring, helping, supporting, tolerant, romantic husband, providing her with safety and security. He will understand her needs, talk to her, and listen intently to what she has to say.

So why do we have trouble even in our Christian marriages today? Because we often view people as secularly and as selfishly as the world does. We enter marriage just as we enter most of our other relationships—wondering what the other person's going to do for *us*.

A new pastor comes to our church, and what do we think? Our first thought is not, *How can I help him?* Usually it's, *How can he help me?* Examples are many, but it is enough to say that our fallen natures and our world system tell us something about people that is totally and tragically untrue: that people exist mainly for our personal peace and pleasure.

God's Truth About People

What, then, is the truth about people? Since we can't get away from people, we might as well learn to live biblically with them. If we are going to recapture our minds for Christ concerning people, we need to learn how to think differently about them, to hold kingdom values, and live out our right decisions.

In Matthew 22 we find a classic passage concerning the great expectation God has for our lives as they concern other people. We have already learned in the preceding pages that the key to true happiness is delighting in and meditating on the law of God. So we should start not with a raft of rules or a pile of principles but with a simple command of God, which our Lord considered to be of utmost importance.

The Pharisees asked Jesus Christ a question. Verses 34-38 read, "But when the Pharisees heard that He had put the Sadducees to silence, they gathered themselves together. And one of them, a lawyer, asked Him a question, testing Him, 'Teacher, which is the great commandment in the Law?' And He said to him, '"You shall love the Lord your God with all your heart, and with all your soul, and with all your mind." This is the great and foremost commandment.'"

Where should our thoughts begin concerning people? In a biblical sense, in order to have a well-ordered, straight life, we must start by loving the Lord our God with all our hearts. Then, because we can't separate God from His creation, the Lord goes on to say in verse

39, "The second is like it, 'You shall love your neighbor as yourself.'" Notice, it doesn't say, "You shall use your neighbor for yourself."

According to God's Word, the truth about people is that they are to be loved—period! That's the biblical command about people. It's precisely the opposite of our fallen instincts. It's directly contrary to the secular advice we receive. But it will be a dramatic statement of the light in the darkness about us.

FEELINGS—OR CHOICE?

Let us make sure we understand what loving others means. The heart of the command is "You shall love." In the text the same word is used in regard to our response to God. In other words, *love* is the key action word in my relationship with God as well as in my relationship with other people.

The word for "love" is the Greek word *agape*. *Agape* is not a word of emotion; it is a word of volition. That means God wants a *volitional,* not emotional, response to people. It is a choice, not a feeling. And we can thank God for that because most of us are still working on our emotional responses to some people! Quite frankly, I find that I can't always control how I feel about many *things,* let alone how I feel about people.

Wouldn't it be tragic, then, if God had commanded us to feel good about everybody? That would be impossible for two reasons. First, we're never going to feel good about everybody we meet or know. There's no way that's going to happen. And second, had He commanded us to feel good about everybody, we would end up continually frustrated, since we simply cannot always control the way we feel.

Some mornings I wake up and, quite honestly, don't feel good about anything. But at those times, I remember that God has not commanded me to feel good about everybody. I can choose to love others as a choice, as an act of my will. In fact, every time God gives us a command in Scripture, He focuses on the volitional aspects of our thoughts and choices. We can always choose to obey, whether we feel like it or not.

Agape love means being willing to meet the needs, interests, and concerns of others. It means being willing to take our resources and contribute them and share them for the benefit of someone else—no matter how it affects us.

Where did we get that definition? John 3:16 is a good start. "For God so loved the world . . . " Did the world have a need? Absolutely! We were hopelessly, helplessly, lost and held captive by sin. We could do nothing about it. It was the love of God alone that met our most desperate need. Do you think God felt good about this fallen world or this fallen race or the death of His dear Son? No. But as an act of His will, He chose to reach out to us. For God so loved this needy planet and these needy people that He *gave*. He shared the infinite resources of Himself in the person of His Son to die and to satisfy our needs. It was perfect, holy selflessness toward others.

Romans 5:8 tells us the same thing. "But God demonstrates His own love toward us, in that while we were yet sinners, Christ died for us." God has literally put on display His *agape* love, center stage at the cross. He gave Himself for us. That is *agape*. It is commitment; it is a choice to be others-oriented, to measure the resources of our lives and to be willing to use those resources to meet the needs and concerns in the best interests of the people around us.

We can choose to do that, whether we feel like it or not. That's the command of God's Word. That's the truth about how to treat people.

WHO IS MY NEIGHBOR?

The text goes on to say that we should act this way toward our "neighbor." But who is our neighbor? Both in the Old Testament (Christ is quoting an Old Testament command) and in the New, our neighbor is anybody who crosses our path. From the people most intimately connected to our lives (spouse, children, parents, work associates), to the next-door neighbor across the fence, to the woman sitting at the red light doing her nails so that we miss the green light, our neighbor is anyone whose life intersects with ours.

My wife often sends me to the grocery store to get one of those "last minute" items. I'm usually glad to do it—that is, until I choose the checkout lane marked "10 items or less, cash only." Invariably, I get behind some "neighbor" who has stacked his or her cart with at least seventeen items—and is writing a check. I normally don't do well in those situations. I don't say much, but I certainly communicate in other ways—with facial expressions, clearing my throat, turning my back, and so on.

But in essence, God is saying, "Stowell, did you ever stop to think that maybe this dear person, this 'neighbor' in front of you, is having a dinner party for eighty people and only needs seventeen more things at the last minute? Did you ever consider that there might be a very good reason he can't afford to take the time to stand in the other line? Did you ever think that perhaps you should be more interested in him and his problems than in yourself?" Of course, those thoughts are rarely the ones that cross my mind at the time.

According to Scripture, that person is my neighbor. I should formulate my thoughts about and construct my operational conclusions regarding that person on the basis of *agape* love. What a difference it would make if I would do that!

WE REALLY DO LOVE OURSELVES

Notice what Christ says next: "You shall love your neighbor as yourself" (22:39). The Bible makes an accurate assumption here. We do love ourselves. Many of us immediately protest, "No, not me! You don't understand my background. My self-image has been shredded. I've been to twenty counselors, and they've told me that my problem is that I don't love myself enough."

If we didn't love ourselves, why would we go to counselors to begin with? If we didn't love ourselves, why would so many of our actions each day (eating, hygiene, selecting clothes, going to doctors, and so on) be dedicated to the sole purpose of caring for ourselves? As long as we live and breathe, we will have a basic drive to take care of ourselves and to meet our basic needs. Sometimes we may not feel good about ourselves, but we do love and care about ourselves.

So in what way do we love ourselves? We love ourselves instinctively, instantly, eagerly, and tenderly. When some felt need marches through our hearts, we immediately want to meet that need and take care of it, don't we?

I'll never forget the time I was trying to fix a hair dryer at home. The hair dryer vents had become clogged, so I thought I would just take the dryer apart and fix it. I took my screwdriver and placed it down the recessed shaft to the head of the screw—but I could not make the screw budge. My next option was to try a pocket knife with a long, skinny blade. I set the knife at the head of the stubborn screw. Then I applied all my energy to turning the knife.

Suddenly the pocket knife folded up against my finger and sliced it nearly to the bone. Blood was pouring out of it. Immediately, instinctively, I ran to the kitchen to wash out the wound and care for my injured finger. The whole family, like baby ducks following their mother, came running after me. They turned the water on while I coached them, "Not too hot; not too cold." Somebody grabbed the bandages, and I urged, "Don't put it over any hairs—I don't want to rip it off later and suffer the agony." On and on it went. Why did I go to all that trouble? Because I am no different from you. We all naturally take care of ourselves because we all basically love ourselves and seek to meet our own needs—instinctively, instantly, tenderly, and eagerly.

That is why God set self-love as the standard of how we are to love others. If you wonder how we are to think about, care about, and love other people, think about the way you treat yourself; then treat others like that. That's the command. That's God's truth about people.

Can we see how different it would make us in a dark, self-centered culture if we cared for and contributed to others in the same way we care for ourselves? What a dramatic expression of light in darkness that would be. We would be set apart by the wonder-working, life-changing power of the truth of God's Word. We would experience exactly what Jesus Christ prayed for, if only we would submit ourselves to this truth.

POINTS OF TENSION

As soon as we say that we are willing to obey this command, we will run into several tension points. One of the first will be *things*. Things have a way of eclipsing the importance of people. Think about a life dedicated to the accumulation of things. It is not difficult to see how easily even those closest to us can be ignored, trampled, and forgotten in the headlong pursuit of material possessions.

I thoroughly enjoy working in my yard. I've got my own system of fertilizing my lawn, cutting it, and caring for it. One year, when my son Joe was in his early teens, I spent all spring getting the yard to look just the way I wanted. We had a basketball hoop at the end of our driveway, and on several occasions Joe came along and said, "Dad, let's play basketball." My response was always, "Joe, not right now. I'm busy working in the yard." Or, "I've got to trim this edge here." Or, "I've got to do the fertilizing now."

Later that summer, I visited a hospital on several successive nights to comfort a family whose boy—about Joe's age—was dying. One evening as I drove home, it struck me that I had a boy just like that, that it was a great gift from God to have a healthy young son, and that I had permitted things—a *lawn*—to eclipse the value of time with him. I drove down our street and saw my beautiful, green, wonderfully manicured lawn. I could hardly stand to look at it. It was a source of sorrow, not joy. I drove into the driveway, saw the basketball hoop, and thought, *I don't care what I have to do tonight; one thing I'm going to do right now is play basketball with my son.*

So I threw open the door and yelled, "Hey, Joe! Let's play basketball!" And he said, "Not right now, Dad—I'm busy." I was convicted, and I wondered, *How could I ever have let things eclipse the importance of my son?*

When you think about the truth about people, beware the treachery of the seduction of things.

If things don't get you, *self-indulgence* may. It's that "me-first" attitude inside all of us that is fanned in our narcissistic culture. When we drive down a congested street, do we ever think of backing off and letting another driver in, just to practice selflessness and love? We've said that the biblical definition of love is the willingness to be others-oriented and to share our resources for the needs and best interests of others. Can we put that into practice when we've just been cut off in traffic, or when we're running ten minutes late and can't stand another interruption?

The bottom line is this: the opposite of biblical love is not hate but self-centeredness. It's hoarding instead of giving, being concerned about self instead of about others. In order to be committed to biblical behavior toward people, to be lights in the darkness, we must be willing to make self servant, not king.

If things and self-indulgence don't eclipse the light of loving others, *scars* might. Many scars in our lives are the result of being ravaged by people, of past pain and abuse. One day we took that step to open up and share ourselves with someone—and he or she dragged us through the shredder and left us in pieces. So we said, "Never again!" We built walls around ourselves, and those ever-present scars keep us from living according to God's truth about people.

I love the story of Joseph. Few men in history have been so greatly scarred by people—by intimate friends and family, no less. His brothers purposely sought to ruin his life; and yet Joseph is a graphic example of how to forgive. When his brothers feared he would take their lives in revenge, Joseph said, "You meant evil against me, but God meant it for good" (Genesis 50:20).

Paul's great discourse in Romans 12 concludes with this exhortation: "Never pay back evil for evil to anyone. Respect what is right in the sight of all men. If possible, so far as it depends on you, be at peace with all men. Never take your own revenge, beloved, but leave room for the wrath of God. . . . If your enemy is hungry, feed him, and if he is thirsty, give him a drink" (vv. 17-20).

That is genuine love. We must guard against letting past pain embitter, separate, or imbalance us in any way. We must not let past scars keep us from obeying God. We need to keep in mind God's sovereignty and glorious power, and in the midst of trials know that He can take the worst things in our lives and turn them into something good and glorious.

Even if no other obstacle trips us up in our pursuit of righteousness regarding people, *people* themselves will. Frederick the Great is reported to have said, "The more I get to know people, the more I love my dog."

People are strange, aren't they? Different. Unique. Aggravating. They don't understand us. They ignore us, use us, climb on us, and heap guilt on us. People, in general, are unpredictable commodities.

A friend told me a story about a lady who was shopping in a local mall. She decided to take a break, so she bought a newspaper and a Kit Kat® bar and sat down on a bench to relax and enjoy her paper and candy. She started looking through the newspaper, and then she broke off a corner of the Kit Kat bar and popped it into her mouth. A nicely dressed gentleman was sitting next to her, and much to her chagrin he suddenly reached down, took a piece of the candy bar, and popped it into his mouth!

The woman was a bit nonplussed, but she figured, *I'll ignore it.* So she took another piece of the candy bar—and he took another piece. Then he beat her to the punch and took yet another piece of the candy bar. By this time she was incensed. She grabbed the Kit Kat, threw it in a garbage can, and stormed off through the mall.

A little later in the day, she saw the same man standing in front of a bakery with a donut in his hand. Later she said, "I don't know what possessed me. I'm not this kind of person, but I couldn't resist the temptation. I grabbed his wrist, took a big bite out of the donut, and walked away." Then she confessed, "When I got home, I put my things down, opened my purse—and there was my unwrapped Kit Kat bar!" All that time she had been eating his candy bar!

Isn't that just like people? We are quick to judge and so prone to misunderstand each other. We get terribly mixed up, and we make relationships tense and complex.

THE ULTIMATE COMMAND

Given the trouble people cause, we are likely to find ourselves thinking, *What would motivate me to follow through with the command to love others as I love myself, considering all the tension people cause around my life?* What *does* it take to ignite our lives with the light of Christ's command? What will it be that convinces us to incorporate that command into the way we think, form our conclusions, direct our decisions?

What is *the* reason we should love people? First, let's consider what are definitely *not* reasons for loving people. It is *not* because certain people deserve it. If that were the case, there would be a great many people we would not need to love at all, because they don't deserve it. And it's *not* because people are nice and lovable. Our wounds and scars assure us that is not the case. Rather, Scripture teaches us that we are to love people because we love God. We love people as an expression of our love for Him.

Remember, in this passage the first and second commandments are inseparably united. Jesus said, "'You shall love the Lord your God with all your heart, and with all your soul, and with all your mind.' This is the great and foremost commandment. And a second is like it, 'You shall love your neighbor as yourself.'" If we obey both orders, Christ says that all the rest of what He expects of us will automatically take care of itself.

Talk about simplifying the Christian life! Jesus commanded two things, and He said that if we get a handle on those two things, we'll please Him in all we do.

Notice that the first requirement of righteousness is to love (*agape* love) God Himself. Again, we are not going to *feel* like loving God every moment of our lives; but we can make a choice to yield to His best interests rather than serving our own. That means submission, granting Him His place of sovereign authority in our lives, and obeying Him. That is what it means to love God.

Jesus Christ said on more than one occasion that He knows we love Him if we do the things He commands us (John 15:10). The biblical demonstration of our love for God is to obey Him, yield to Him, and be concerned about Him and His agenda for our lives. He says in essence, "If you love Me, here's what I want you to do, first and foremost: love people." Of course, our response to that is usually, "Lord, don't start there! You don't know the people I know. I'll tell you what. I'll be a missionary. I'll double-tithe. I'll sell Bibles on the street corner. I'd be glad to prove I love You in a hundred other ways, but please don't make me start with people!"

But God says, "If you really yield to Me in love, then the first thing I want you to do is to reach out and love people."

The Father's Prized Possession

We can say we love God. We can sing that we love God. We can teach Sunday school, sing in the choir, memorize Scripture, learn theology, and raise a Christian family. But God says that the proof of our love for Him is the way we treat others. The first item on His agenda is to love people. That's how important people are to Him. They are God's number one priority in the entire world. Not buildings. Not church programs. Not missions budgets. Not publicity. God's most pressing heart priority and interest is people.

Why? Because people were created in His image. People will live forever. Indeed, mankind is fallen, but God redeems us through the death of His dear Son. The Son of God spilled His precious blood for people. There's nothing in this world more important to God than people. People are His precious creation and the precious objects of His redemption.

How can I say I love Him and not be concerned about the same things He is concerned about? How can I say I love Him and not have His primary interest at heart? How can I say I love God and not seek to treat people the way God seeks to treat people—with fairness, justness, righteousness, mercy, grace, understanding, forgiveness, patience, and forbearance?

Since people are precious to God, they should be precious to me. If everyone is precious to God, then everyone must be precious to me—not because people deserve to be precious on their own merit but because they are precious to Him.

We love people because we love God and seek to please Him. This is the motivation that fuels the light of our torches in regard to people—regardless of what people may be worth to us.

When my parents moved to southern Florida, they sorted through some of the family treasures and divided them among the children. My dad brought me a little box and said, "Joe, I want you to have this." When I opened the box and pulled back the cotton, there was an old pocket watch—one of those round ones that usually hangs from a fancy gold chain with a watch fob on it.

I have a few antique clocks, so I was somewhat aware of the value of old timepieces. That watch did not have a famous maker's name on it, or a brass or gold or sterling case; it did not have a fancy gold chain or watch fob. In fact, it was really a common old watch with a leather thong tied to it. As a watch, it was not something of great worth.

But my dad said, "This was the first watch I ever owned. My dad gave me this watch." I remembered that he and I used to fish the St. Joe River every summer, floating down the river and fly fishing in the evening. This was the watch he used to pull out every once in a while to see what time it was.

You know, if my dad had taken that watch to an antique store, they would have told him it was worth little, if anything. But all the money in the world couldn't buy that watch from me. That watch is precious to my father, and since it is precious to him, it is precious to me.

That's what people are like. That's why God in essence said, "Love Me? Love people!"

In John 13:34-35, as Jesus prepares to be parted from His beloved disciples in order to give His life for a lost world, He says, "A new commandment I give to you, that you love one another, even as I have loved you, that you also love one another. By this all men will know that you are My disciples, if you have love for one another."

God never intended people to be controlled, used, abused, manipulated, climbed upon, withdrawn from, or ignored. He intended that people be loved—as He loved them; as we love ourselves. Because we love Him and seek to please Him we will treat that which is precious to Him as precious to us.

This is the way Christ's disciples are to think about all people, and this is the way that we will light the darkness of a crass and careless culture.

As our world fans the flame of self-centeredness, elevates the worth of things, and treats people carelessly, as though they had no worth, Christians who love regardless will be a beacon to which many alienated and lonely people will come.

Love dramatically lights the night.

9

A FATAL DISTRACTION

Getting Prosperity into Perspective

It had been a long time since I had read a comic book, so as we walked into the restaurant I couldn't resist picking up the Donald Duck edition from the stack the manager had placed near the door to entertain restless children.

I enjoyed the step back into my past, particularly the colorful character of Scrooge McDuck, Donald's miserly uncle, whose top hat and cane are outdone only by the dazzling diamonds in his tie tack and the jewels dripping from his fingers.

At one point in the story, Scrooge McDuck enters his treasury room, a warehouse stacked deep with dollars, coins, and gems, and dives head-first into his riches. He proceeds to wallow in his wealth. The epitome of success, he has more money than he knows what to do with.

The scene seemed so intriguing to me. It was then that I realized that it was no longer the little boy in me enjoying the comic book—it was the grown-up man who momentarily felt the seduction of the world's abundant prosperity.

That is not unlike what happens in our country when we conduct state lotteries. Recently, the Illinois state lottery reached a total prize of 78 million dollars. That meant that one lucky person (who had paid only a dollar for a little ticket with numbers on it) was suddenly set for life. Like Scrooge McDuck lounging atop his riches, the lottery winner was the person through whom thousands vicariously enjoyed the ultimate dream come true.

Why does Scrooge McDuck's swimming in his treasures, or a 78 million dollar lottery winner, or a publisher's sweepstakes payoff appeal to us? Because money has our world in a stranglehold. It has a way of stealing our hearts. We want to make it, save it, spend it, and possess it. We live in a world where, for the most part, there seem to be only two kinds of people: those who are rich and those who want to be rich. We live in a world where money isn't everything—but whatever is in second place is far behind.

THE PROBLEM OF PROSPERITY

If you sometimes feel guilty for feeling tempted by prosperity —don't. It is not wrong to prosper, nor is it wrong to want to prosper. What is wrong, however, is our *concept* of prosperity. Our problem is that we think prosperity is measured in dollars, vacations, cars, houses, social circles, and status. The problem with our longing for prosperity is that we have defined it incorrectly.

It may come as a great surprise that God Himself has planted in our hearts a longing to prosper. If we miss the true sense of prosperity, then we will long and live for the wrong stuff.

Quite frankly, the cause of Jesus Christ has received a knockout punch from the fallen definition of prosperity. Because our longing for prosperity has been tragically misdefined, the Body of Christ in North America is reeling back with dollar signs in its eyes and charge cards circling over its head.

Needless to say, worshiping in the temple of temporal gain requires some significant sacrifices. Our families suffer as the darkness seduces us to prioritize gain above spouses and children. We spend our energies on extra work and double incomes and relegate our children to day-care centers and latchkey status. When the day is done our energies are spent, and having given our focus to material gain, there is little left to pour out at home. The residuals from this sacrifice are significant.

The strength of the work of Christ is compromised as well. The promise of quick credit and plastic cash leaves us in bondage to debt and unable to support the kingdom. When we prioritize financial and material gain, our energies, time, and talents are exhausted on the realm of empty treasures where, as Christ said, "moth and rust destroy, and . . . thieves break in and steal" (Matthew 6:19).

Thus, there are few "leftover" resources to support the kingdom of God because our understanding of prosperity has encouraged us to heap it all—time, talent, and treasure—upon ourselves. As we near the next millennium, we must ask, What about the next generation? We are told that fifteen thousand missionaries are going to retire before the turn of the century. Who's going to replenish those troops? All over North America young people are encouraged to choose their careers based on what they enjoy, how they can make the most money, and what will help them achieve their parents' standard of living as quickly as possible. What of the legions of workers that will be needed to win the world to Christ? Who will go? Who will send them? In short, our false sense of prosperity threatens to weaken the supply line for eternity.

There is a crying need for us to enhance our families, Christ's cause, and eternity by living according to God's definition of prosperity. Thinking rightly about and living for biblical prosperity are essential to penetrating the darkness with Christ's light. Rather than discounting the desire for prosperity, we must read the signs correctly so that we may enjoy the prosperity God offers to all of us.

MYTHS ABOUT PROSPERITY

In order to understand true prosperity we must define and deny the myths that seduce our minds from the truth.

LIFE CONSISTS OF PRESENT GAIN

Recently, a national retail chain advertised its products with the slogan "There's more for your life at Sears." That statement reflects the essence of our cultural mind-set, which claims that life consists of the accumulation of things. If the advertisers had said there's more for your house, cottage, car, lawn, and hobbies at Sears, the jingle would have been more accurate. But does life itself consist of possessing an abundance of things? The darkness says yes. So does the bumper sticker that facetiously claims "the one who dies with the most toys wins."

In Luke 12 we encounter one of the Bible's most powerful passages concerning this false concept of prosperity. The text is alive with drama.

As Jesus Christ walked through the crowd, one individual caught His eye and pressed a question. If you had one "live" interview with Jesus Christ, what question would you ask Him?

The text states, "Someone in the crowd said to Him, 'Teacher, tell my brother to divide the family inheritance with me'" (v. 13).

Can you believe it? One chance to talk to the Lord, and he wants bucks instead of blessings! He wanted temporal gain instead of timely, life-changing insight. This man's brother had cheated him out of some money from the family estate, so he went to Jesus to ask the Lord to guarantee his income. It is amazing that we can become so preoccupied with money that things of spiritual importance are overshadowed. This man brought to Christ his dollar-laden heart and asked for material gain.

Jesus Christ responded, "Man, who appointed Me a judge or arbiter over you? . . . Beware, and be on your guard against every form of greed; for not even when one has an abundance does his life consist of his possessions" (vv. 14-15). The King James Version says, "Take heed, and beware of covetousness: for a man's life consisteth not in the abundance of the things which he possesseth."

What a profound statement! Throughout Scripture, God warns us against a covetous heart and the seduction of living and lusting for the immediate fulfillment of material passions. He warns us against the covetousness that finally takes life and lays it upon the altar of monetary gain and material gratification.

Covetousness is that fixed focus that always wants more and is willing to do whatever is necessary to gain it. It's the outlook on life that says, "I want it, and I must get it regardless of the cost." Covetousness is the opposite of contentment, the godly satisfaction the Bible so highly values.

According to Jesus, true prosperity begins with believing that life consists of more than the things money can buy. To drive this pivotal point home Christ told the story about a certain rich man whose land was very productive. "And he began reasoning to himself, saying, 'What shall I do, since I have no place to store my crops?' And he said, 'This is what I will do: I will tear down my barns and build larger ones, and there I will store all my grain and my goods. And I will say to my soul, "Soul, you have many goods laid up for many years to come; take your ease, eat, drink and be merry."' But God said to him, 'You fool! This very night your soul is required of you; and now who will own what you have prepared?'" (vv. 15-20).

This is a penetrating commentary on a life dedicated to wealth. Here is a man whom our world would regard as the ultimate success; he was wise, clever, and blessed. Yet from God's point of view he was a "fool" because that night he would stand before God. Though he had been rich by man's standard, by God's standard he was impoverished. An old Spanish proverb warns, "Shrouds have no pockets." And Chuck Swindoll has said, "I have yet to see a U-haul in a funeral entourage headed to the cemetery."

Temporal wealth, rather than *eternal riches*, had ruled the life of the man in the parable. His actions had been dictated by his desire to generate income, increase profits, manage investments, and achieve the kind of success our world so highly values today. Unfortunately, he had chosen to serve the wrong master. As Christ said, "What will a man be profited, if he gains the whole world, and forfeits his soul? Or what shall a man give in exchange for his soul?" (Matthew 16:26).

The principle is clear: the claim that the essence of life is monetary and material gain is a myth, whereas true prosperity is being rich toward God. It is investing today in that which lasts forever.

Christ then turned to His disciples to rescue their minds from the same trap the rich man in the parable had fallen into. He said, "Do not be anxious for your life, as to what you shall eat; nor for your body, as to what you shall put on. For life is more than food, and the body than clothing" (vv. 22-23).

Though the disciples were not rich, their hearts could be seduced to live for even basic gain—a better meal, a better pair of sandals. That, too, would be a fatal distraction from living for the prosperity of gain for Christ's kingdom. Christ assured them that since God clothed the lilies and fed the ravens, He would certainly care for their needs. This knowledge releases us to be focused on gain for Christ, trusting Him to meet temporal needs.

He concluded, "And do not seek what you shall eat, and what you shall drink, and do not keep worrying. For all these things the nations of the world eagerly seek; but your Father knows that you need these things. But seek for His kingdom, and these things shall be added to you. Do not be afraid, little flock, for your Father has chosen gladly to give you the kingdom" (vv. 29-32).

It is not a matter of what you have or don't have. It is not a matter of what you get or don't get. It's a matter of where your focus and attention are fixed. Those who truly prosper live for spiritual, kingdom gain in their homes and in the marketplace. With their dollars, time, energy, and talents—whether they have little or much—their priority is to invest in God's kingdom.

THE DOLLAR HAS ULTIMATE WORTH

Traveling in Canada is a grand economic experience. There is a great rate of exchange—for us in the U.S., that is. But I've also traveled in England, and that is a terrible experience in terms of the rate of exchange. Whether traveling in Canada or in England, the pivotal issue is, "What is the dollar worth today? What is the rate of exchange?"

From the perspective of God's kingdom, the question is far more significant. How does the value of a dollar affect our thought processes as Christians? Does the desire for a fine house and a fat raise take precedence over our family's needs as we consider a new job or a promotion? Does the vision of a beautiful new building or a lucrative fund-raising campaign reorder the priorities of our church or Christian institution? Does the potential of quick and easy income tempt us to compromise our commitment to Christ and His Word? Is the value of a dollar worth more than anything else, or are some things in life more important?

The might of the inflated worth of the dollar is tragically revealed in the heart of Christ's disciple Judas. A close study of Judas's life reveals his tragic flaw to be a misperception of the worth of cash. Although this temptation is common to the entire human race, it is a lure that overwhelmed and destroyed Judas.

According to Luke 22:1-6, at the end of Christ's ministry Judas went to the religious leaders and said, "I will deliver the Messiah into your hands for crucifixion." Then he negotiated a deal for the head of the Messiah in exchange for thirty pieces of silver. In essence, financial gain was far more important to Judas than a loyal relationship with Christ Himself.

In John 12 we have a clear insight into Judas's primary motivation in life. It's important to remember that Judas didn't flip out in the last few weeks of Christ's ministry. He didn't suddenly go berserk over money. Rather, within Judas' heart was a consistent, misplaced priority regarding the value of cash.

In John 12:1-3 we read, "Jesus, therefore, six days before the Passover, came to Bethany where Lazarus was, whom Jesus had raised from the dead. So they made Him a supper there. Mary therefore took a pound of very costly perfume of pure nard, and anointed the feet of Jesus, and wiped His feet with her hair." Mary took her most prized possession—a pound of perfume called "spikenard." This costly oil was gleaned from tiny plants, which were picked by hand and crushed. The oil was then transformed into a precious ointment with a beautiful fragrance. The text tells us Mary owned a pound, and in that day a pound of spikenard was worth about a year's wages. How much do you make in a year? Whatever your annual income, that's how much the spikenard would have been worth to you.

What did Mary do with this precious commodity? She took it, and she went to Jesus, saying in essence, "I do not know how else to tell You how much I love You!" Christ had just raised her brother from the dead, and undoubtedly she was overflowing with an inexpressible sense of gratitude and worship. It was as though she wanted to say, "Lord, I value You more than anything else in my life— even more than the value of this perfume!" Then she broke the bottle and anointed Christ's feet with it. What a beautiful expression of love and worship!

Then Judas entered the picture: "But Judas Iscariot, one of His disciples, who was intending to betray Him, said, 'Why was this perfume not sold for three hundred denarii, and given to poor people?'" (v. 4). John, writing this gospel after he had found out about Judas, includes a revealing editorial comment in verse 6: "Now he said this, not because he was concerned about the poor, but because he was a thief, and as he had the money box, he used to pilfer what was put into it."

Soon after he heard Christ say that He was going to the cross and that the world would persecute the disciples, Judas left. He went out, sought the scribes and Pharisees, and negotiated thirty pieces of silver for betraying Christ. He did so because cash was more important to him than a loyal, uncompromised relationship with Christ. He had traveled with Christ for three years with that eating away at his heart. Today we have people in our churches who have gone through the motions as "Christians" for years but have never altered their misplaced priority of cash over Christ.

Some believers give to the cause of Christ simply because they believe "you can't out-give God," and, if they give a lot, God is going to give a lot more back. Though it's true that we can't out-give God, there isn't a worse reason in the world to give to Christ. What will happen if He doesn't give it all back to us? Will we bail out at that point as Judas did?

There are times when businessmen join prestigious evangelical churches simply for the business contacts they can establish. Some Christians unfairly litigate, cheat on taxes, strike unethical business deals, and violate their conscience and their relationship with Christ for cash.

When I was first in the pastorate, I was asked to speak at a banquet in another state. You can't imagine how prestigious I thought that was. I now had an "interstate ministry"! I couldn't wait to put it on my resumé. I drove to that other state and spoke at the banquet, and afterward I waited around for the emcee to hand me an envelope with the expense check and honorarium in it. I waited around until everybody was gone. I helped fold up chairs. I said good-bye to him in every way I could think of. He kept saying, "Good-bye, have a nice trip," but no envelope was forthcoming. Finally, I got into my car and drove home.

I got in at 2:00 A.M., and the next day I said to my wife, "I drove all the way up there, and they never asked about my expenses. They never even mentioned an honorarium." I grumbled about it in my heart and in my mind. I even waited for it to come in the mail. But it didn't come that first week, and it didn't come the second week. Sometimes it takes a long time for God to get through my stubborn brain, but finally the Spirit of God convicted me. "What are you in this for? Are you in this for money? Did you go up there for an honorarium? You went up there for bucks?" I had to say, "No, Lord. I'm not in this for money. I'm in it for You."

I prayed, "Lord, never again will I minister for money. I'll work for Your kingdom and trust You to care for my needs." It was a hard lesson for me to learn.

The next day the check came in the mail. But I had learned the lesson that I needed to serve God, not money.

Why are you in this thing called Christianity? Is a relationship with Christ more important to you than any amount of money? Tragically, that wasn't true of Judas, even though he passed as a disciple of Christ. Some are tempted in the business world to "cut a deal," even though they have to deny their commitment to Christ. But everybody does it, so it must be OK. If you have to break your fellowship with Christ to make an extra dollar, you need to ask, Is a dollar or a thousand dollars really worth more to me than Christ?

What Mary knew and Judas didn't know was that a relationship with Christ—worship, gratitude, and obedience—is far more valuable than even a whole pound of spikenard. It is worth more than a year's wages—or even a lifetime's. Be careful of the seduction of the dollar. True prosperity is eternal fellowship with Christ, unhindered and expressed in worship and grateful obedience.

So it is a myth to consider the dollar something of supreme worth. Though it can be a legitimate means to a godly end, money is never an end in itself or a means to an unrighteous end. Rather, money is always worth less than children, spouse, relationships, the advancement of the cause of Christ, a clear conscience, or investments that last for eternity.

THE WICKED ARE BLESSED BECAUSE THEY PROSPER

The third seductive myth is the prosperity of the pagan. Somehow it seems unfair when God appears to reward the schemes and evil ways of the godless with prosperity and permits so many of His own to have so little. The seduction plays out in scenes of believers who end up scheming like the pagans to prosper, or in the lives of those who won't compromise to gain but still end up feeling cheated and embittered because God is so inequitable. After all, "If God is good to anybody, shouldn't He be good to me? I've been so good to Him!"

In Psalm 73 we find the author of the psalm, Asaph, reeling because he has watched the pagans around him prosper while he has lived in want.

In the poetic style of the psalms, this psalm begins with the conclusion: "Surely God is good to Israel, to those who are pure in heart!" This is the issue of Psalm 73. Asaph had passed through a season in his life in which he had doubted God's goodness.

In verse 2 he says, "But as for me, my feet came close to stumbling; my steps had almost slipped." He says, in essence, "I almost lost it all in this prosperity issue because I was envious of the boastful when I saw the prosperity of the wicked."

He goes on to describe them. "There are no pains in their death" (v. 4). In other words, they have enough money to be comfortable all the way to the grave.

"They are not in trouble as other men" (v. 5). Literally, they can buy their way out of any problem, and they're not plagued by creditors.

"Therefore pride is their necklace" (v. 6). They are cocky and arrogant.

"Violence covers them like a garment." They get away with all kinds of things. They cheat in the marketplace. They cheat on their taxes. They have enough money to manipulate other people. They're violent, lawless people.

Verse 7 observes, "Their eye bulges from fatness." This is especially graphic. Have you ever eaten so much that you feel like your eyes are bugging out? The psalmist says that these people have so much to eat that their eyes bulge with abundance. They're stuffed! They have more than their hearts could ever hope for, just as in our country some people have so much money they don't seem to know what to spend it on next.

"They mock, and wickedly speak of oppression; they speak from on high. They have set their mouth against the heavens, and their tongue parades through the earth. Therefore his people return to this place; and waters of abundance are drunk by them. And they say, 'How does God know? And is there knowledge with the Most High?' Behold, these are the wicked; and always at ease, they have increased in wealth" (vv. 8-12).

In verses 13-14 the psalmist has a "pity party" because of the prosperity of the wicked. He writes, "Surely in vain I have kept my heart pure, and washed my hands in innocence; for I have been stricken all day long, and chastened every morning." He's saying, "It's not fair. I've been innocent all my life, I've lived for God, I've lived the godly life. And all I get is chastening and a bucket full of trouble. It's just not fair!"

In verse 17 he says, "Until I came into the sanctuary of God; then I perceived their end." What is the solution to being seduced by the prosperity of the pagan? How can we properly adjust our thought processes? By looking at it from God's point of view. Go into the sanctuary of God. Get close to God, and let God give you His perspective. The psalmist said he finally went before God with his problem, and God opened the doors of understanding. "Then I perceived their end." He allowed God to teach him that in reality the wicked ultimately have no prosperity at all.

What is the end of the unrighteous who are wealthy by the world's standards? Verses 18-22 say, "Surely Thou dost set them in slippery places; Thou dost cast them down to destruction. How they are destroyed in a moment! They are utterly swept away by sudden terrors! Like a dream when one awakes, O Lord, when aroused, Thou wilt despise their form. When my heart was embittered, and I was pierced within, then I was senseless and ignorant; I was like a beast before Thee." In essence he is saying, "Lord, I'm so ashamed. I forgot what the end of their lives would be like when they face You, the holy, almighty God, having lived their pagan ways in rebellion against You. They will taste fair judgment for their sin."

In simple terms, it's somewhat like a baseball game. What difference does it make if you have one big inning but lose the whole game? The psalmist stretches our thoughts beyond the here and now to eternity. He helps us understand that prosperity is measured by standards beyond this life, not just by the things we accumulate. That's exactly what Christ confirmed when He urged, "Do not lay up for yourselves treasures upon earth, where moth and rust destroy, and where thieves break in and steal. But lay up for yourselves treasures in heaven, where neither moth nor rust destroys, and where thieves do not break in or steal; for where your treasure is, there will your heart be also" (Matthew 6:19-21).

The psalmist then revels in the essence of true prosperity. "I am continually with Thee; Thou hast taken hold of my right hand. With Thy counsel Thou wilt guide me" (vv. 23-24).

He continues in verse 24, "And afterward receive me to glory." Hell is canceled and heaven gained.

He concludes, "Whom have I in heaven but Thee? And besides Thee, I desire nothing on earth. My flesh and my heart may fail, but God is the strength of my heart and my portion forever. For behold, those who are far from Thee will perish; Thou hast destroyed all those who are unfaithful to Thee. But as for me, the nearness of God is my good; I have made the Lord God my refuge, that I may tell of all Thy works" (vv. 25-28). True prosperity is the presence, protection, and guidance of God and the eternal guarantee of heaven.

As the writer of Hebrews states, "Let your character be free from the love of money, being content with what you have; for He Himself has said, 'I will never desert you, nor will I ever forsake you,' so that we confidently say, 'The Lord is my helper, I will not be afraid. What shall man do to me?'" (13:5-6).

The story is told of a missionary couple's return home from years on the field. On the boat with them was an important, wealthy man and his wife. The missionary observed the drunken and crude behavior of this famous passenger. When the boat docked, there was a band to meet the rich man, crowds of adoring friends, and flowers for his wife.

As the missionary couple picked their way alone through the crowd, unnoticed and ungreeted, the wife said, "We've lived our lives for Christ. We've given everything we had. Now we've come home, and you deserve to have someone here to meet you for what you've done for Christ. I'm not selfish, but there are no flowers here for me."

Her husband looked at her and said, "But, honey, we're not home yet." He understood what true prosperity is all about. He was willing to live now in the light of eternity.

The prosperity of the wicked is not a sign of God's blessing on them. It is His grace, if anything. Though we may have little, we have the goodness of God bestowed upon us in His presence, protection, guidance, and assurance of eternal reward in heaven. We have true prosperity.

PROSPERITY IN PERSPECTIVE

Biblical thinking about prosperity, then, resists the seduction of secular myths regarding the essence of life, the worth of money, and the seemingly good wages of sin. The authentic Christian concludes that prosperity is found in investing for the kingdom as we trust God to meet our temporal needs, pouring our lives into commodities that are worth more than the dollar, and rejoicing in the prosperity of Christ's presence and His provision for our eternity.

True prosperity sees beyond the material things and checkbook balances of today and instead values that which is spiritually significant and eternally strategic.

CONTENTMENT, COMMITMENT, AND CONSECRATION

In 1 Timothy 6:6-19 Paul summarizes the essence of the light in the darkness of monetary and material seduction. Three dynamic principles emerge.

First, *godliness, with contentment, equals gain for Christ* (1 Timothy 6:6). Unfortunately, many Christians rewrite the formula and read, "Godliness plus gain equals contentment."

Contentment does not mean we never need, want, or desire anything. It is that settled peace that says, "If I can't have it in the context of biblical priorities and purposes, then I can live happily without it." Contentment keeps our passions fixed on things of eternal importance as we resist preoccupation with temporal gain.

The second truth that transforms our tendency toward the temporal is a commitment that, if we are to pursue anything, *let us pursue godliness.*

The text warns, "But those who want to get rich fall into temptation and a snare and many foolish and harmful desires which plunge men into ruin and destruction. For the love of money is a root of all sorts of evil, and some by longing for it have wandered away from the faith, and pierced themselves with many a pang" (vv. 9-10). Instead, we are admonished: "Flee from these things, you man of God; and pursue righteousness, godliness, faith, love, perseverance and gentleness. Fight the good fight of faith, take hold of the eternal life to which you were called, and you made the good confession in the presence of many witnesses" (vv. 11-12). True riches are measured in character, in who we are—never in what we have. We are to focus on becoming rich in these commodities that honor Him and bring light to a darkening world.

But what of committed Christians who have been blessed of God with earthly abundance? It is important to note that Scripture does not command those who have much to feel guilty or to deny it all for the "simple life." It is their responsibility, however, to *consecrate all they have to Christ* and not to be deceived by their possessions. Timothy provides five guidelines for those who do prosper materially and seek to be consecrated to Christ:

1. Avoid conceit (v. 17). If driving that nice car makes you feel or act superior to others of lesser means, then change your attitude or sell the car. Any sense that what I have makes me worth more than others who have less is pagan to the core.

2. Keep hope fixed on God (v. 17). The temptation to trust in our wealth or possessions, to become self-sufficient, to not pray, "Give us this day our daily bread," is spiritually lethal. Trust God, not the "uncertainty of riches." A good test is, How would I respond if I lost it all? Would it be traumatic or promote a continued trust in Him?

3. Enjoy the gifts of God (v. 17). If God has blessed you, learn to enjoy what He has given without guilt or apology. He "richly supplies us with all things to enjoy." It's interesting how we quickly apologize for the things we have. If we feel true guilt for something we have, we should get rid of it. If not, we should enjoy it as a gift from God.

4. Be rich in works, not wealth (v. 18). If your bank account were made up of the good works you have deposited on behalf of Christ and others, how much true wealth would you have?

5. Be generous (v. 18). Do less fortunate people in your world share in the benefits of the temporal gain that our Lord has seen fit to grant you? Does the cause of Christ blossom because of your giving spirit?

Paul then concludes that the rich are to "[store] up for themselves the treasure of a good foundation for the future, so that they may take hold of that which is life indeed" (v. 19).

One couple my wife and I know has been blessed with abundant wealth. They are exceedingly generous to God's cause and the needs of others, giving sacrificially of their strength, their time, and their resources. They are like missionaries to the wealthy of their community. Their possessions do not possess them, but they have consecrated their resources to good works and eternal gain. Once, when Billy Graham came to town for a crusade, they catered a dinner in their home for wealthy friends, rented a bus, took the group to the crusade, and brought them home for a dessert buffet and a discussion of the claims of Christ.

A biblical view of true prosperity neither bashes the blessed nor beleaguers the bereft. It really is not an issue of what you have but of what has you. It is not a matter of what you own but of how much our Lord owns of your mind and heart concerning what He has given you. Prosperity is being rich toward God in terms of present godliness and an enriched eternity.

Do we know what prosperity is? According to Scripture, ultimate prosperity is measured in terms of eternal investments and eternal gain. It is the presence of God in our lives. It's when He holds us with the power of His right hand, no matter what happens, like a father who holds the hand of a little child as they walk down the street. If the child stumbles and both feet go flying out from under him, he still has the stability of his father's strength.

To those of us who have come to know Christ and are indwelt by His Spirit, genuine unshakable prosperity is the guiding, helping, protecting presence of Christ. If you have Him, you have it all!

10

CREDENTIALS OR CHARACTER

Success in the Light of God's Word

After hearing the word for a long time I finally found out what a nerd is. There in the barber shop was a full-length poster depicting this cultural statement of personal disaster. It was a picture of a guy carrying an overstuffed, well-worn briefcase. He had short suit pants (my children call them "floods"), white socks, dark scuffed shoes, no jacket, "fly away" collared white shirt, a clip-on tie that was too short, and masking tape on his crooked glasses. In his shirt pocket was one of those industrial plastic pocket protectors with eight or nine pens sticking out of it.

As the barber clipped away I found myself intrigued with the poster. Why would it sell? Why would anyone hang it up? Why did it seem so interesting, clever, and funny? Then it dawned on me that this was a cultural statement about what success doesn't look like.

In a world seemingly gone mad in portraying successful images, willing to do almost anything to at least appear successful, this guy makes us all feel good. Compared to him most of us in the barber shop had our act together. Even a bad haircut looked good compared to his.

Outside of the need for physical provision I don't know of a stronger urge in our souls than the urge to succeed. Whether it's success in business, at home, in relationships, or just as an individual, the desire to succeed and to be recognized for our success is woven tightly into the fabric of our being.

And it does not always need to be spectacular. Sometimes we feel successful just having survived the day. We want to be successful persons, parents, husbands, wives. We want our business to succeed and our plans to succeed.

Success is not a dirty word. The surge in our souls for success is present in all of us. God has planted it within us that we might be driven to be successful for Him and enjoy the satisfaction of true success.

So the challenge lies not in our interest in success but rather in how we define success. What is our operational definition of this desire?

Defining success is critical because it is a force that ultimately establishes the direction of our life and shapes our future. If, for instance, I believe success is making a million dollars, then I will set the agenda and course of my life to achieve that goal. It will dictate my career choice and the expenditure of my time and energy.

Since success is such a basic, directive force within us, it should come as no surprise that the prince of darkness would like to alter the way we think about success and establish his own operational conclusions, that we might be misdirected and serve his purposes.

He has been eminently successful. Even Christians of long standing will say that success is reflected in the car you drive, where you live, what your income is, where you go on vacation, who you know, who you are seen with, what clothes you wear, as well as how much position, power, and prestige you have. Pastors and church leaders often talk of success in terms of building programs, size of congregations, books written, degrees obtained, places spoken at, and positions in the church or denomination.

On the contrary, even the most successful of us in terms of these definitions of the darkness may well be abject failures, not only before God but in life itself. Granted, not everyone is ambitious enough to want to grab the gold at the top of the ladder. For some of us, it's enough just to know peace, comfort, and companionship and to enjoy life around us. As innocent as that sounds, if we call that success, we, too, have succumbed to the definitions of the darkness.

Secularism's definition of success claims that true success is attaining what is best for me and drives me to set my life goals to get it.

UNDERSTANDING SUCCESS

Success, regardless of its goal, is driven by three dynamics: power, position, and praise.

POWER

Whether it's the power to achieve my personal success or the lust for power over others that comes with success, power is a significant lure in the drive to succeed.

All of us have power. Even the poorest and most afflicted of us have the power to elicit responses of mercy, sympathy, and pity. If we are clever enough, we can even use that power to manipulate others to guarantee some success.

All of us have some power just by virtue of height, weight, position, quickness of mind, sharpness, or knowledge. If the boss abuses Fred at work, Fred may come home and take it out on his wife, who may then scream at one of the kids, who then beats up on his little brother, who then kicks the dog, who then bites the cat, who hops onto the table and eats the goldfish.

Even our words have phenomenal power. Some time ago I read a testimonial about the power we possess just in the words we speak. Listen to what this person says about his life:

"My junior high school had scheduled its annual production. Talented students were quick to try out for the various parts. I was not so certain of my abilities and had decided that singing in an operetta really wasn't for me. Then Mrs. Wilson, my music teacher, asked me to try out for the role of a servant. It was not a coveted role, but it did have three solos. I am certain that my audition was only mediocre, but Mrs. Wilson reacted as if she had just heard a choir of heavenly angels. She said to me, 'Oh, that was just beautiful. That was perfect. You are just right for the role. You will do it, won't you?' And I accepted on the spot."

He continued, "When the time came for the next year's operetta, most of the students who had played the leads the year before had graduated, and Mrs. Wilson had transferred to another school. In her place was a rather imposing figure who had an excellent singing voice and a sound knowledge of music theory. As the tryouts began, I was ready. I felt confident that my talent was just what the operetta needed. With approximately 150 of my peers assembled, I really felt that everything would go well. But, if I live for an eternity, I will never forget the words spoken to me that day. When my audition was completed, the teacher said, 'Who told you you could sing?'

"The timid youth of a year earlier was suddenly reborn. I was totally destroyed. Harsh words are bad enough under any circumstances, but to a young, idealistic boy, they can be devastating. From the time those six words were stated, it took eight years and the coaxing of my fiancée before my voice was ever raised in song again."

We all have power simply because we're people. Some of us have the power of personal resources, such as the resources of our spiritual gifts or the resources of our material treasures, and those personal resources make us power brokers in the world around us. Others, as we have already said, have been granted position, and with position comes worldly power.

The difference between legitimate and illegitimate use of power is the way in which our power is directed. Is it self-directed or others-directed?

Ultimately, there are no powerless people. One issue in coming to grips with a righteous sense of success is, "How do I use the power I have, and what will I do with the power that success may bring?" If my power is used to accomplish self-centered goals of success, particularly to the harm of others, and then used to maintain and guarantee my success, then I have ignored the very purpose for which God gave power in the first place.

POSITION

Success is defined as well in terms of the positions that we hold. When I was a child I played King of the Mountain. The point of the game was to see who could stand on the top of the hill the longest without getting knocked down. We still play the game as adults. It's a little more complicated now and is played with symbols that represent where we fit on the slope of the mountain. External credentials establish position: the size of our house, the number of cars in the garage, the title on our business card, the floor our office is on, the jewelry in the safe, and on the list goes.

Periodically, I ride the train to work. I enjoy watching the executives take their places and flash their symbols, as we all try to out-pinstripe each other. Briefcases establish position. Pens we use, shoes we wear. Middle management wears button-down shirts, and upper management plain collars. Of course, the quintessential symbol of position is to spend the whole train ride doing business over your portable phone.

We even establish position in casual social encounters. If someone is pointed out across the room we ask, "And what does he do? Where does he live?" If I introduce you to my friend Bob, I say, "I want you to meet Bob. He's a doctor at St. Luke's." If I don't tell you his position, there's a good chance you will ask him what he does shortly into the conversation.

Position is vital to a system of secular success. But it is relatively insignificant in the biblical pursuit of authentic success.

PRAISE

Once secular success is attained in terms of the prestige of power and the credentials that establish position, its coveted reward is the affirmation and praise of others. Some of us no doubt believe that if we could be "successful," others would envy our accomplishments and affirm our worth and value. Success enables those who have arrived to bask in the praise of others, who almost covetously wish they, too, had arrived. It certainly says a lot about the shallowness of the secular system when we establish and affirm worth by external credentials and accomplishments.

Yet all of us have an intrinsic need to be affirmed and to receive the praise of others. Being a pastor is a vulnerable position on Sunday mornings. After spending most of the week agonizing, forming, and shaping a sermon, you finally deliver your heart. As you walk through the foyer afterward, you can't wait for the parishioners to tell you how God used your words in their lives. You slow down to hear whether they are affirming your message. And you hear, "Did you hear Swindoll last Friday? Wasn't he great?" So then you can't wait to get in the car because your wife's going to tell you how wonderful it was. You drive all the way home, but she's quiet. You think, *Well, she's waiting for the right chance*. But when the praise is not forthcoming, you start throwing out all kinds of hints. "How did you like Sunday school today?" "How did you like the music in church?" "How did you like the choir?" Actually, you don't really care how she liked Sunday school. It doesn't make any difference! You're just waiting and hoping for some hint of praise!

Mom needs praise after she prepares a successful meal. So does dad after risking his life to clean gutters. And so do the children on a regular basis for the small successes in their lives. Often we look to success as the means of gaining the praise of others.

Again, the need for praise is not inherently wrong. It is intrinsic to our being. But the direction of the secular mind-set distracts us to seek praise in a false system of success.

ULTIMATE SUCCESS

Those of us who are committed to resisting the intrusion of darkness into our minds must understand the dramatic danger of having the wrong operational conclusion about success. Commodities such as families, relationships, and the cause of Christ are suffering tragically because of the secular success syndrome. It places tremendous stress on every important area of our lives and is most often disappointing, leaving us, even when success is attained, empty and still searching for fulfillment.

It tempts us to violate ethical and moral commitments and troubles our conscience. Often when we do succeed, we've paid far too high a price for the glory and we feel like a failure inside. We try to climb the ladder only to find it's leaning against the wrong wall.

Authentic biblical success is both attainable and fulfilling. With it comes no hangover of regret or sense of inner failure. Christ dramatically reordered our thinking about success in a strategic encounter with His disciples recorded in Matthew 20:20-28. The stage was set as James and John came with their mother to ask Christ for a personal favor. Mrs. Zebedee wanted her two sons to be one on His right and the other on His left when He came into His kingdom.

In a monarchy, such as this would be, the two most powerful people, next to the king himself, would hold these positions of power and praise. She simply wanted her sons to be successful. What mother doesn't? Yet the problem for this mother was that her success would be the attaining of these prestigious and powerful positions for her sons.

Obviously, James and John agreed with the request; they came with her. They hoped that they would be the ones to carry the credentials of power and position and that they would receive the praise of others.

Christ responded by reconfiguring their mind-set about success. It was His goal to plant biblical thinking, and subsequently, biblical living, in their heads regarding success.

First, Christ asked them if they were willing to suffer with Him (v. 22). That's a strange way to qualify a person for success, yet Christ knew that even the success of God's plan for redemption would demand His ultimate suffering at the cross. Some of God's most eminently successful people have found that success comes with doses of difficulty. In fact, James 1 clearly indicates that our success as individuals is often precluded by a measured amount of suffering.

As God lists the heroes of the faith in Hebrews, He cites not only those who were apparently successful in this life but also those who were

> tortured, not accepting their release, in order that they might obtain a better resurrection; and others experienced mockings and scourgings, yes, also chains and imprisonment. They were stoned, they were sawn in two, they were tempted, they were put to death with the sword; they went about in sheepskins, in goatskins, being destitute, afflicted, ill-treated (men of whom the world was not worthy), wandering in deserts and mountains and caves and holes in the ground. And all these, having gained approval through their faith, did not receive what was promised, because God had provided something better for us, so that apart from us they should not be made perfect. Therefore, since we have so great a cloud of witnesses surrounding us, let us also lay aside every encumbrance, and the sin which so easily entangles us, and let us run with endurance the race that is set before us, fixing our eyes on Jesus, the author and perfecter of faith, who for the joy set before Him endured the cross, despising the shame, and has sat down at the right hand of the throne of God. For consider Him who has endured such hostility by sinners against Himself, so that you may not grow weary and lose heart. (Hebrews 11:35–12:3)

Authentic thoughts about true success do not exclude trauma and trouble. Clearly, success is not just that which is comfortable and convenient. To be successful, doesn't necessarily mean we are "carried to the skies on flowery beds of ease while others fought to win the prize and sailed through bloody seas."

Next, Christ made clear that legitimate places of power and prestige are given by God in His sovereign plan and time, not grabbed by persons greedy for the privilege (v. 23). Biblical success is attainable for everyone, not just the quick, strong, or first in line. Yet when God needs someone to serve in an elevated position, He elevates His selection. And often it is the unlikely, like David the little shepherd boy. One tragic outcome of success is that so many who strive to come out on top become frustrated and disappointed when it doesn't work for them. The truth is that God seeks those who have become successful in His eyes, though perhaps lowly in man's estimation, to promote to trusted positions. Young David had a heart for God.

Those who do grab for gain, even if they get it, cause dissension and strife. At this point in the text, the other ten disciples hear about the request and become livid with anger (v. 24). Why? Simple. They, too, had hoped for success, and James and John had beat them to the punch. Remember, these men were among the most committed men this world has ever known. Yet reigning in their hearts was the desire to be "king of the mountain." Not one of us is exempt from the desire or delusion of secular success.

Christ reproved the disciples for their pagan thoughts about personal success. He said, "You know that the rulers of the Gentiles lord it over them, and their great men exercise authority over them" (v. 25).

It is clear, then, that Christ expects us to function differently in terms of success for He concluded His reproof by saying, "It is not so among you" (v. 26).

Having concluded that self-serving definitions of success are of this world system, and having called us to a "different ethic," Christ then defined success in terms of authentic greatness among people of the kingdom. He stated, "Whoever wishes to become great among you shall be your servant, and whoever wishes to be first among you shall be your slave" (vv. 26-27). Here is the dramatic difference. Christ's kind of success is the loyal dedication of my life and heart to serve Christ and others. In the kingdom, "the way up is down." Note that Christ did not reprove the disciples' desire for success. He simply redirected their thinking about what it is. In fact, He held Himself up as the model, saying, "Just as the Son of Man did not come to be served, but to serve, and to give His life a ransom for many" (v. 28).

Success in God's eyes has nothing to do with credentials and has everything to do with character—in particular, the Christlike character of servanthood. Authentic success dedicates itself to the success of others by serving their needs and enabling them to grow and prosper, just as Christ came to serve my needs and gave Himself to me to guarantee my success against sin.

What then of position, power, and praise—those elements of secular success that we are so addicted to? What about people who have by God's hand been privileged to hold rank and who possess many of the credentials of earthly prosperity? In and of themselves, position, prosperity, and power, and the glory they may bring are not inherently evil. Many fine Christians who are truly successful in God's eyes have been blessed with much and hold many earthly symbols and credentials. But the issue is not who we are or what we have. The issue is what our operational conclusion about success is.

If one who has much materially says, "By God's grace I have much, yet that does not make me a successful person," he's on the biblical track.

If he lives to effectively serve Christ and others with all his heart and resources and makes that claim his goal for success, he is truly great in God's eyes, regardless of who he is or what he may or may not have.

In fact, no one has ever equaled the power and position nor built the resources that Christ did. According to Philippians 2:5-9, He used His power to empower us to salvation, good, growth, and glory. The only legitimate use of power is to empower others to what is good and upright.

The power of our words, talents, spiritual gifts, experiences, skills, position, and prosperity (or lack thereof) becomes illegitimate power the moment we use it to empower ourselves for personal advancement.

Paul says in Philippians 2:5-11 that the power God has given us is transferable. We give it away to empower others. Could Christ have used His power to demand that all the world serve Him? Absolutely. Instead, however, He took His power and used it to ultimately empower other people. He empowered us for that which is good, for growth into His likeness, and for eternal glory. Therefore, we can rightfully conclude that biblical power is the empowerment of others for their good, their growth, and His glory.

NOT A THING TO BE GRASPED

This concept of success is not difficult to understand, but it *is* a difficult concept to live consistently. It is uncomfortable and inconvenient to use our power to empower others when they don't seem to deserve it, which is exactly why we need to anchor our thoughts in Philippians 2. This passage reveals how Christ Himself took the power of His eternal glory and transferred it from Himself to us.

Verse 6 says, "Who, although He existed in the form of God, did not regard equality with God a thing to be grasped." "Grasped" literally means to cling to. This text is not talking about Christ's releasing His divinity; rather, Christ, the eternal Son of God, did not consider the privileges and prerogatives of being God something to be held tightly or used only for Himself. He was willing to let go that He might empower others.

In fact, the word *emptied* in verse 7 can be understood in more than one dimension. We can not only view this as the pouring out of His divine privileges and prerogatives; it may also be understood that He poured Himself out *to others*.

Therefore, in order to think biblically about the power God has given us, the first thing we must be willing to do is be like Christ. "Have this attitude in yourselves which was also in Christ Jesus," the text admonishes us (v. 5). "This attitude" meant the attitude that yielded His privileges, plans, and dreams that He might be released to empower others.

What are your privileges? What are the comforts of your life? What are the prerogatives you hold on to? Do you hold these so tightly that you will never let go to empower another person?

Consider the story of the Good Samaritan. When the question was asked, "What does it mean to love your neighbor?" Jesus Christ told the story of a man who was ambushed by thieves and left in a ditch. Two power brokers walked by the victim that day—a Levite, a priest—religious people who possessed buckets of power. They walked by, clinging to their power and refusing to empower him.

In contrast, along came the Samaritan, who also had an abundance of power—the power of time, resources, and prestige. We don't know where he was going that day, but it is unlikely that he was just out for a nice walk in the springtime. He probably had someplace to go, something to do, plans and dreams of his own. Maybe he had worked hard for his money and his donkey. They were *his* privileges, prerogatives, perks, and possessions. Yet suddenly, in that moment of someone else's need, he was willing to give up his plans for that day. He yielded the silver in his purse and his means of transportation. He gave it all up to empower another person.

Jesus Christ would never have used His divine power for our good if He had not been willing to give up His privileges and prerogatives as God. In the same way, you and I will never live biblically and willingly empower others as long as we cling to our power tightly.

Jesus' position as God was used to help us understand our lost state and our need for a Savior. In fact, in His majestic position as God He assumed the form of a servant and humbled Himself all the way to the cross for us (Philippians 2:7-8).

Whatever position God has given us—whether parent, husband, wife, foreman, teacher, executive, or friend—can you imagine the dramatic impact of our saying, "I will use the influence of my position to serve the best interests of others for their good, growth, and the glory of God through their lives"? That is true success.

When I first came to work at Moody Bible Institute, a well-meaning friend said, "You really took a step up." But no. There are no "steps up" in the kingdom. It is a vast vineyard, and we are all servants sovereignly assigned to our places in His field. As such I am called to serve Christ and to do everything in my power to serve students and associates, urging them toward what is truly best for them. To use the power and position God has given for personal gain is to abort and distort God's appointment.

Success is not measured in credentials but in the character of Christ reflected in our lives. It is measured in our servanthood. It is not in our power or position but in how we use our power and position. It is not in what we have but in how well we serve with what we have. That is why Paul began this passage with the words "Have this attitude in yourself which was also in Christ Jesus" (Philippians 2:5).

But what of our need for praise and affirmation? It is realized in that glorious moment when we will hear from our Lord, "Well done, thou good and faithful servant. Welcome into the joy of the Lord." This alone is the ultimate affirmation and the pinnacle of success.

11

WHAT IS GOD WORTH?

Dispelling the Darkness with True Worship

What is God worth to you?

Don't answer too quickly. What is He really worth to you? And how does anybody else know what He is worth to you?

This is a particularly crucial issue in light of the secular environment that regularly bombards us with the message that God at best is irrelevant and worth little, if anything. The darkness enlarges the worth of pleasure, possessions, comfort, self-indulgence, and affluence and devalues the essential worth of God.

One grand statement that messengers of the light can make is that God is the ultimate object of worth. We can show this through our thoughts, statements, and, ultimately, our actions. Unless, that is, the worth of God has been discounted in our own thinking.

Somewhere between tipping our hats to God on Sunday morning and missionaries' shedding blood for the cause of Christ, we regularly make statements about what God is worth to us. How? Through what we call "worship."

In our own language the word *worship* comes from the root word *worth*. Thus, worship is the ongoing declaration of the worth of God in my life—all that I am and do because of all that He is and does. It is the "worth-ship" of God.

A traditional favorite at Christmastime is the classic film *Little Lord Fauntleroy*. When the film opens, little Fauntleroy is being raised by his widowed mother in the slums of Boston. His father was an English aristocrat who had married an American and was therefore disowned. After he was killed in the war, his widow and young son were left to fend for themselves. However, one day his grandfather in England, realizing that apart from his grandson he had no heir, set out to find his grandson in America. He finds the boy and elevates little Fauntleroy from the slums of Boston, where he played kick-the-can with his friends, to the English aristocracy. From slum child to Little Lord Fauntleroy—he is dressed up and paraded through the streets. To his surprise, both servant and merchant bow and say, "Good morning, your lordship."

How much more does the Lord Jesus, as He walks through the streets of our lives, deserve our respect. It is right and proper—it is our obligation, in fact—to bow before Him and say, "Good morning, your Worth-ship." What is God worth to you? Does anybody know? That is the measure of worship.

As we consider worship, we need to recognize that our thinking in this area has been radically affected by the world around us. And the way we think about worship has affected our operational conclusions concerning worship, which in turn, have affected the decisions we make and the way we practice our worship. What a tragedy it would be for us to be given this wonderful privilege and yet not understand what it really means. Or, worse yet, to be seduced by the myths of darkness that lead us into false worship or to not even know the means God has given us for proving His worth. As we reorder our thinking, we need to let God teach us the meaning of the myths and the means whereby we worship Him.

Romans 12:1 is a text that leads us to a fresh understanding of and a revitalized commitment to worship. Whereas some might point out, as is often stressed, that this verse deals with the principle of dedicating our lives entirely to Christ, the overarching emphasis is worship. Dedication is but one aspect of worship, of proving God's worth. If we don't see the worship thrust here, we miss the point of this passage. If we base our life dedication on this verse but it is not rooted in the reality of worship toward God, our dedication may be shallow and short-lived.

What does worship mean? Paul wrote to the church at Rome, "I urge you therefore, brethren, by the mercies of God, to present your bodies a living and holy sacrifice." Don't miss the fact that Paul calls for a *living* sacrifice, not a sin sacrifice. The sacrifice for sin has already been made. Rather, the type of sacrifice referred to in the verse is the worship of Almighty God. The metaphor draws our attention immediately to worship.

In terms of worship, there is a dramatic shift from the old covenant to the new covenant. We live in the new covenant sealed by the blood of Christ at the cross, and our worship now is based on different terms. In the Old Testament God's people worshiped in a place—the place where God dwelt. It was filled with somber, purified priests, vessels that had been set aside, and rituals of cleansing and appropriate approach to God. It was all external. In the new covenant, however, God instituted a tremendous change. Now God dwells in our bodies (1 Corinthians 3:16-17; 6:19). We have become His temple! Now who are the priests who manage the system of worship? According to 1 Peter 2:9, *we* are believer-priests. How many of us realize what has happened to all those Old Testament vessels, which were prepared to be used in worship to God? Second Timothy 2:21 says that our bodies are like vessels intended to be purified for use in God's service.

New covenant worship takes place intimately in us and through us. So when this verse says we are to take our lives and place them on the altar, we are doing so as an act of worship to God—a privileged, personal responsibility that takes place in our lives.

This text also instructs us that worship is a response to God. The first word in the verse, "therefore," is a transition from the preceding eleven chapters of clear, deep instruction concerning the redemptive work of God. Hell was formerly our portion—and it was a fair portion at that. But God, in His redemptive work, reached down and touched helpless, hopeless persons like us. He cleansed us of our sin and lifted us up. Hell is shunned and heaven is gained for those who receive Him by faith.

In response to the wonderful, redemptive work of God, then, what can we do, how can we say thanks? Paul answers with the word "therefore." Worship is a response. It is never exercised in a vacuum; it is always a response to God.

What kind of response should our worship be? First, and foremost, it is a *required* response. From the beginning, God has required worship. When God gave the Ten Commandments, the first requirement for a life that pleases Him was "You shall have no other gods before Me" (Exodus 20:3). That's a worship command. We are to singularly focus our worship on God alone. Worship is a required response.

Second, worship is a *qualified* response. Notice that Romans 12 says we are to bring our bodies as a statement of worship to God, as "holy." Remember that the vessels used in Old Testament worship had to be purified before they could be used for worship to God. We must be the same—in life, in mind, in body. The extensiveness of this holiness includes every aspect of our beings. Holy for God. It is a qualified response.

Third, we can see that worship is to be a *priority* response to God. Don't forget the context of Romans 12. In response to the first eleven chapters and God's statement of our redemption, we will offer our lives as a sacrifice in worship to Him. We will also let Him transform our minds. Then we will serve the Body of Christ with our gifts. We will live godly lives.

If we had time to do only one thing for God, what should we do? Worship God! If we understand what God has done for us, worship will be our top priority.

LIVING STATEMENTS OF WORSHIP

Notice that the text tells us to present our bodies as *living* statements of worship. I have a friend who says that the problem with living sacrifices is that they keep crawling off the altar. That is a problem, but the point of this passage is that, in contrast to the dead sacrifices of the Old Testament, we are to worship God alive! We are to worship with life, with all the living fiber of our beings.

A few years ago friends were coming to visit for the weekend. At that time God's provision kept us very close to the survival line. Those were precious days, as God proved Himself to be a faithful provider. As we thought through what we had available to serve our treasured friends for dinner, did Martie say, "I've got one can of peanut butter, and I've got some good strawberry jam. How about if we buy some bread and lay out a little buffet and let them make sandwiches"? Of course not! Instead—though we could barely afford it—we stretched our resources for our friends. We weren't trying to impress them, but we wanted to say something to them. We wanted to tell them how much they meant to us, how much they were worth to us. So we found a butcher in town who sold us some prime rib of beef. We made baked potatoes and broccoli with cheese sauce. It was a sacrifice for us to do that—but our friends were worth it. We stretched ourselves to make a statement.

How many of us are willing to make a similar statement concerning God's worth in our lives? He says, "Behold, I stand at the door and knock; if anyone hears My voice and opens the door, I will come in to him, and will dine with him, and he with Me" (Revelation 3:20). When we let Him in, what does He find on our tables? Those things from our lives that are convenient and comfortable? Or do we stretch our resources every day to demonstrate how much He is worth to us? That's what true worship is all about.

Would we stretch to say no to a less than honorable business deal to publicly state His worth? Live on a lower scale to have more time, energy, and money for Him, His cause, or our family? Would we give up a career for Him? Give up our children to His service? Resist the temptation for gain or gratification to show that He is worth more than those things to us? Refuse to fall to the seduction of sensual lusts to make a statement that He is worth more than they are?

MYTHS ABOUT WORSHIP

Our problem may be that many of us have been misdirected by the *myths* of worship. If we are going to make any progress, we have to learn how to set aside those myths and think clearly about worship.

What are these worship myths? Some of us mistakenly believe that worship is a warm feeling we get when the music is right, the service is right—when everything is right in church. We walk out and say, "Wow! *Did* I worship today!" We conclude that worship is a feeling.

But that's wrong. Although worship may include feelings, it is not primarily emotional. Worship is a *choice*—a choice to express how much God is worth to us. We can thank God that there are times when worship does produce feelings, and we can express to God how we feel. But on those days when the feelings just aren't there, we can still worship God through concrete expressions of His value to us.

Another myth claims that worship is a place, or a set time, or a formal liturgy. We come to the point where we equate worship with a set of routines, like divine hoops we jump through to do our church thing. Think about a typical Sunday morning. When we should be getting ready to express to God how much He is worth to us, we're reading our bulletins or thinking about what we need to do that week. Or we're criticizing the youth department because they're doing things we never did when we were that age. Or we're thinking about what's happening in the church that we don't agree with, crumpling up our bulletins and folding our arms in defiance. Then the service begins, and as somebody tries to release us from the bondage of this world and direct us to God by asking us to sing "Amazing Grace," we grumble, "Didn't we sing that three weeks ago? They sure don't have much creativity around here." The pastor prays his pastoral prayer, talking to the one God who is worth it all, and we think, *How much longer will he pray, anyway?*

Then comes the time to demonstrate how much God is worth to us by publicly giving of our resources. Regardless of what we claim He is worth up to that point, it now becomes clear that He's not worth a whole lot. There is a story about a $20 bill and a $1 bill. The twenty said to the one, "I go everywhere: the finest restaurants, the opera, the islands. How's it with you, One?" The single replied, "Church, church, church. All I ever see is church!"

As the service continues, we have the opportunity to express God's worth to us by listening attentively to Him through His Word. But as the message is proclaimed, people begin looking at their watches after twenty minutes. Then, of course, at noon all the wristwatch alarms go off.

God may well weep at eleven o'clock on Sunday morning. Indeed, too often it can be said of us—just as Isaiah said to Israel and as Christ said to the Pharisees—"You hypocrites, rightly did Isaiah prophesy of you, saying, 'This people honors Me with their lips but their heart is far away from Me'" (Matthew 15:7-8).

Yet worship is much more than a place, an act, or a ritual. Worship happens intimately and corporately. Worship is loud, and worship is soft. Worship is public, as well as private. True worship is worship through tears and laughter. True worship is through grief and joy. Worship is asking every day and everywhere, "How can I prove how much God is worth to me?"

MOTIVATION FOR WORSHIP

Once we have established the meaning of worship and have set aside the myths, we must begin to understand that God has given us great motivation for worship. He is worth our everything because He has redeemed us. He is fully worthy of the living sacrifice Romans 12 admonishes. He has redeemed us; therefore, we can say, "Lord, here's all of me." That's the capacity to truly worship!

In God's Word we learn that the children of Israel crossed the Red Sea while the Egyptians sank like stones when God let the water rush back. What did the Hebrews do on the other side? They worshiped God—with song and timbrel and cymbal and dance! The intervening, redeeming work of God was their motivation for worship.

Actually, some of us may feel that God hasn't done enough for us, and therefore our motivation to demonstrate His worth runs a little thin. I'm reminded of the time I asked a professional baseball player how he handled the fickleness of the crowd: one day a hero, the next day trade bait. He said that a long time ago he learned that the fans are interested in only one thing: "What have you done for me today?" It has been said that if God has done nothing more than redeem us from sin and hell, He has already done infinitely more than we deserve.

When we lived in Detroit, we used to love to go to the stadium and watch the Tigers play ball. The problem with Tiger Stadium, however, is that it has support posts, and when there is a full house there is always a chance of getting a seat behind one of those posts. Well, when I went to a playoff game in 1984, I couldn't wait to get there. But when I arrived, I was seated right behind a post. All I could see was that post, and it was rather dull and discouraging. In fact, without a clear view of the game, I soon lost my enthusiasm for it. It's that way for a lot of God's people. We sit behind the post of our own concerns or our own dreams, and we lose our view of God. We no longer see God at work in everything, and thus we lose our enthusiasm and capacity for worship.

When we see Him in all that is around us—in good times as well as bad, in sickness as well as health—the momentum and enthusiasm will begin to accrue. When we see God at work, our hearts will be lifted in worship. After all He's done for us, how can we do less than give Him our best and live for Him completely?

Our Resources

Not only do we have sufficient motivation through His redemptive work, we have as well the resources and capacity for worship. Those resources are abundant: time, talents, energy, attention, finances, possessions, mind, voice, and body. Unfortunately, we limit those resources severely through the tyranny of a busy schedule, misplaced priorities, and misspent minds, talents, and checkbooks.

The sacrifice to God on the altar of our lives will include praising Him in song, testimony, and word and yielding ourselves to purity and service. It will mean giving God the credit everywhere and all the time. And it will mean adopting His thoughts as our thoughts, His concerns as our concerns, and His conclusions as our conclusions.

I'll never forget the night I ministered on the island of Haiti to a packed-out church of about five hundred Haitians, who stood together and sang a hymn to God. I recognized the tune, and though the language was not familiar, anyone could tell that those people loved God and couldn't wait to express that with their lips. It wasn't a professional performance—for the most part they were dreadfully out of tune; there was no alto, tenor, or bass; nobody said, "Now, the ladies on the next verse." But it was one of the most beautiful things I've ever heard because they did it with such sincere gusto for God. It was the sacrifice of praise of their lips.

Another example of verbal praise was shown to me by my Hebrew professor in seminary when he received too much change at the bank. He turned back and said to the lady, "I'm sorry, but you've given me too much."

She said, "My, you're an honest man."

"It's not that I'm an honest man," he answered. "It's that Jesus Christ has changed my life."

How beautiful was that simple act of worship. He gave credit to God and expressed what He was worth.

May God rebuke us for misusing our lips, that altar of praise and worship! Or for using our resources, time, and energy for everything but worshiping Him. Regardless of what our resources are, the Bible actually commands us to worship God with the totality of our beings, which includes everything we own or possess. Why do you sing in the choir? Why are you an usher? Why do you do what you do in the local church? Do you know? If it's for anything less than demonstrating how much God is worth to you, then it's something less than true service and certainly is not worship. True worship is proving how much He is worth, "stretching" our time and talents to say, "God, You are worth this much to me."

WORSHIP EQUALS OBEDIENCE

Finally, we need to recognize that true worship cannot take place apart from obedience. How many times in Scripture is obedience the theme of worship? In Genesis 22, for example, God tells Abraham to bring Him his son in the context of an altar and a sacrifice. He is not asking for a sin offering but for Abraham's worship. God had given Abraham the most precious gift in the world, and now He was testing Abraham to see if the gift had become more valuable to Abraham than the Giver. Obedience was the only way for Abraham to prove that. When we think of all the gifts God has given to us, we have to wonder if we have fallen in love with the gifts and if we have relegated the Giver to second place. So God comes along and says, "Will you do what I ask? Will you give it all up for Me? Will you place it on the altar? Will you forgive that person for Me? Will you stop lying for Me? Will you be an honest businessman for Me?"

What is worth more to me than God? What is more important than showing His worth through my obedience? Why do we say no to temptation? Because we don't want to get caught? No! (Actually, we usually think we are clever enough to get away with it.) The reason we obey God and resist temptation is that our actions are a public demonstration that God is worth more to us than the misdirected passions of our flesh. We resist temptation to demonstrate to God that He's worth more than that. In other words, we worship Him with our obedience.

Of course, that means worship requires unflinching allegiance no matter what. Sometimes we want to worship God on our own terms.

We say in essence, "If You do this for me, then I'll be glad to demonstrate Your worth with my lips, my resources, and my obedience." But what do we do when nothing good is happening to us? What do you do when all the gifts are gone, when life's blows leave us barren?

> Now it happened on the day when his sons and his daughters were eating and drinking wine in their oldest brother's house, that a messenger came to Job and said, "The oxen were plowing and the donkeys feeding beside them, and the Sabeans attacked and took them. They also slew the servants with the edge of the sword, and I alone have escaped to tell you." While he was still speaking, another also came and said, "The fire of God fell from heaven and burned up the sheep and the servants and consumed them, and I alone have escaped to tell you." While he was still speaking, another also came and said, "The Chaldeans formed three bands and made a raid on the camels and took them and slew the servants with the edge of the sword; and I alone have escaped to tell you." While he was still speaking, another also came and said, "Your sons and your daughters were eating and drinking wine in their oldest brother's house, and behold, a great wind came from across the wilderness and struck the four corners of the house, and it fell on the young people and they died; and I alone have escaped to tell you." (Job 1:13-19)

Job—with this entourage of tragic events fully in place—rose and tore his robe, grieved, shaved his head. But then, *he fell to the ground and worshiped!* He said, "'Naked I came from my mother's womb, and naked I shall return there. The Lord gave and the Lord has taken away. Blessed be the name of the Lord.' Through all this Job did not sin, nor did He blame God" (Job 1:21-22). Later, he affirmed, "Though He slay me, I will hope in Him" (13:15).

True worship worships even when all is gone. When all on earth is gone He remains with us, and it is to Him we cling. And we worship by means of unflinching allegiance to Him, regardless of what happens. Why? Because He is in and of Himself worthy of worship.

How much is God worth to you? Who would know? And how would they know?

In the darkness, where God is worth less than almost everything, the light makes a clear and penetrating statement that God, indeed, is worth everything to us.

12

A Call for Compassion

*Responding to the Worth of
Even the Worst in the Darkness*

When I first moved to Chicago, one of the big adjustments I had to make was the commute I faced every morning. Instead of driving twelve minutes to my office, I had to get used to driving at least an hour—*if* I left by 6:00 A.M.!

I had to figure out how to make use of that time. One thing I started doing was reading bumper stickers, and I've come up with a lot of favorites. One of them reads, "If a woman's place is in the home, why am I always in the car?" Another proclaims, "So many pedestrians, so little time!" Then, of course, there are the hostile bumper stickers: "Don't tell me to have a good day!" and, "As a matter of fact I do own the road!" And so on.

A number of years ago the slogans moved off bumpers and onto rear windows. Yellow diamonds began appearing in back windows, and the first yellow diamond issued an important announcement: "Baby on board!" It was a crucial statement, designed to warn people that inside the huge machines of plastic, aluminum, and steel hurtling down the freeway at monumental speeds, was perhaps a precious, valuable, vulnerable baby.

As might be expected, that gave rise to a host of other signs, such as "Ex-boyfriend in trunk!" "Nobody on board!" and others. But then, in response to the original "Baby on board" sign came the reply, "Who cares?" I thought, *How cold can you get? 'Who cares'! Who cares about a precious baby on board?* Maybe it was intended as humor, but it was callous nonetheless.

As I thought about that sign, its spiritual application penetrated my heart like a spear. I thought about those things that are precious to God. I thought about those who are vulnerable in this fast-moving, hell-bound world. I thought about the lost—those who don't know Jesus Christ—and about how precious they are to God. Then I wondered if God looks at my life—even though I'm busy around the kingdom—and sees a big, yellow diamond swinging from my neck that says, "Who cares? Who cares?"

THE WORTH OF PEOPLE

One of the problems in our secularized world is that the worth of an individual is founded on his or her performance. Whether in relationships, business, entertainment, or athletics, the people who perform the best supposedly have the most worth. Conversely, those who are unproductive or countercultural have little worth. As Christians we can easily impose this pagan notion on those who reject Christ, especially those who are blatantly evil.

God, however, tells us that all people have worth in this world—and that includes the lost. When God looks at this world, He attaches great value to the lost. Somehow, we must reclaim the roots of an authentic Christianity, which remind us of that. We need to hear God's heartbeat, change the way we think about the lost, make decisions that will rip the "Who cares?" sign from our necks, and begin to extend ourselves compassionately to those around us who need Jesus Christ.

In Luke 15 three famous episodes vividly illustrate this point. In these episodes we are reminded that we are not the only ones who have struggled with one of those apathy signs. In this chapter Christ tells the stories of the lost coin, the lost sheep, and the lost son (better known as "the prodigal son").

As we examine these stories, we need to remember that Jesus Christ never told stories just to entertain a crowd. When Christ told a story, He told it to make an important point. The point of these stories, in fact, goes straight to the heart of the commission Christ gives us concerning the lost.

In addition, when Jesus Christ told a story, He based it on a setting or a context. Therefore, we will not understand these three stories until we understand the tension from which they developed.

WALKING AMONG THE LOST

Thus, we need to understand the first two verses of Luke 15. In verse 1 we read, "Now all the tax-gatherers and the sinners were coming near Him to listen to Him." Notice the order in which the people are mentioned. In Christ's day, the tax-gatherers were the charlatans of society. They were Jewish by birth, but they had sold out to Rome. The Roman authorities expected them to collect a tax of a certain percentage from the Jewish people, but they were also free to collect any other fees they chose in addition. In short, it was government-approved extortion. In the Jewish mind, tax collectors were the dregs of society. In this context, Jesus Christ was standing in the center of a crowd—maybe in the marketplace or in the outer courts of the Temple. As the crowd gathered around Him, along came the tax collectors.

The "sinners" were also gathering around Christ. "Sinners" is a technical term in New Testament terminology that refers to people who basically had no regard for righteousness or the law of God. They lived as if God did not exist. They had no accountability but simply did whatever they wanted. Unlike in our society, Judaism in that day regarded the law of God and His righteousness as the standard, which meant that "sinners" also were among the lowest people in Jewish culture.

The text tells us that all the tax-gatherers and all the sinners were coming near to listen to Him. As the episode opens, Christ is at the core of this crowd of lost people, who were not just the socially acceptable lost but the really unacceptable.

This has an obvious application to our posture toward the worst in current society. In particular, these people would include ones on the leading edge of today's secularism, which is so hostile toward us. The issue is, *Do we care about them?* Do we pray for them and seek ways to win them to Christ? They too are in need of a Savior. We should applaud the groups working with homosexuals, drug addicts, and AIDS victims. Whether it is aimed at the best or the worst, compassion is the appropriate expression of light to a lost world.

Verse 2 continues to build the tension from which the stories stem: "And both the Pharisees and the scribes began to grumble." Picture the scene: Christ is at the center of the crowd, and as the tax collectors and sinners begin to press toward Him, the "religious" people of the day, the Pharisees and the scribes, come along. They say, "This man receives sinners and eats with them." In other words, "He spends His time with the worst of the lost!"

Why was this such a problem to the Pharisees and the scribes? Because Jesus Christ had claimed to be God, and like some religious leaders today, the scribes and Pharisees wanted to condemn Him for hanging around with the ungodly. This Man who claimed to be God spent time with "terrible people."

That attitude is similar—if not identical—to the wrong thinking of many Christians today. The religious leaders' theology was a "good guys/bad guys" theology, and it was not right theology. Their thinking was that because God was good and perfect, His representatives and His Messiah would hang around only with those who were a part of "the good guys' club." Who did they think were the good guys on earth? Themselves, of course! They assumed that because God is a holy God, those tax collectors and sinners would surely be judged and condemned by Him. Such people were therefore unworthy of time and attention.

Therefore, they reasoned that if Christ were really God, He'd be walking around with the religious crowd, reproving the lost from a distance and pronouncing judgment on them. Instead, this Man who claimed to be the Messiah fraternized with the lost, and that made no sense. According to their theology, God wouldn't have time for the lost. The only thing the lost deserved from God was judgment.

Christ told these three stories to reprove the scribes and Pharisees for their fallen sense of the worth of the lost. He wanted everyone to know the truth that *God values the lost.* Not only did God send His Son to earth, but He sent Him to walk with the lost—because God cares for them.

The religious leaders knew nothing about God's mercy. They only knew that the judgment of God is real. It is true that God is just and must judge sin. He is a holy God, and no sin can stand before Him. The religious leaders were right on that count, but they knew virtually nothing about the wonderful truth of God's mercy and the fact that God deeply loves the lost.

SETTING THE STAGE

Christ told the three stories to make two specific points: (1) God cares for the lost and, therefore, (2) those who claim to know Him will also care for the lost.

Learning this penetrating lesson will reorder our thinking and change the way we operate. First, we need to identify the players in the parables. In all three stories, we need to understand who each character actually represents. In the story of the lost sheep, for example, the shepherd represents God the Father. The lost lamb, therefore, represents the sinner, or the lost individual—the kind of person that made up the crowd around Jesus. In the story of the lost coin, the woman represents God the Father, and the lost coin represents a lost sinner. Finally, in the story of the prodigal son, the waiting father —ready to forgive—represents God the Father. The younger son represents the lost and the elder brother the grumbling Pharisees.

Understanding those roles, then, let us allow the stories to speak to us about why God cares for the lost.

GOD CARES FOR THE LOST

God cares for the lost because God Himself has suffered a significant loss. When we use the word *lost,* most of us think, *They just haven't found their way to heaven. They haven't read the gospel road map. They haven't met a Christian who will show them the way. Once they do, they will cease to be lost, find their way, and go to heaven.* But when we think about the lost theologically, we need to understand that God Himself has suffered a significant loss.

Consider, for example, a shepherd who has only a hundred sheep. In Christ's day a shepherd's flock was his bank account. If a shepherd lost even one of those sheep, he suffered a significant loss.

If a widow has only one small bag of coins to support her through the end of her life and loses one coin, she has suffered a significant loss.

And what about a father who has lost a wayward child? What could be a more significant loss? God cares for the lost because He Himself has suffered a significant loss—the loss of something dear to Him.

Let's put this into the context of Scripture. In Genesis 1-2 we read that God created all things and then stood back and said, "That's good." The pinnacle of that creation was man and woman, whom He created to have fellowship with Him. He created them in His image so that they could know Him and so that His character could flow through them. They would demonstrate to all creation what the invisible God is like.

But in Genesis 3, sin enters and rapes the scene, leaving mankind dead in trespasses and sins and hopelessly alienated from God. That's when God suffered a significant loss because of sin. When Adam and Eve sinned, He could have just vaporized His creation and started over again. But He didn't. Instead, He went back to the Garden and called to Adam and Eve. Once He exposed their sin, He set the precedent of sacrifice to cover sin and redeem that which was lost.

The rest of Scripture, then, is about the way God has chosen to bring the lost back to Him again. It reveals to us how the nation of Israel carries the seed of Messiah. It gives us the history of that seed protection and His arrival at the cross, the empty tomb, and the resurrection. When we get to the end of the Bible, we find a new heaven and a new earth in Revelation 21. Because of the redemptive work of God, we who believe will all be with Him together. John heard a loud voice say, "[God] shall dwell among them, and they shall be His people, and God Himself shall be among them" (v. 3). That which He lost at the Fall will be regained! So great was God's loss that it has preoccupied the entire flow of history. It is of eternal concern to Him. It was the first crisis revealed in Scripture, and it is the last to be resolved. God cares for the lost because when man died in sin God suffered a personal loss.

Many of us have suffered significant losses: a spouse, a parent, a child, a close friend. We know how greatly that hurts. We say, "If I could only have him/her back!" If that is how we feel, imagine the heartbeat of God, who has lost His creation to sin, and how greatly He desires to win them back.

WILLING TO STEP IN

These stories also demonstrate the *proof* that God cares. What is that proof? It is that He was willing to intervene.

The lost are hopelessly, helplessly lost without Him. The shepherd lost his sheep, and that lamb was hopelessly lost until the shepherd intervened. Sheep are not quite up to par mentally. Lambs don't come home by themselves. In fact, if you put them out to pasture, they'll eat the pasture down to the dirt. And if they don't have a shepherd to lead them on or take them home, they'll die of starvation in that dry pasture. Whoever gave Little Bo Peep that famous advice led her astray. "Leave them alone and they'll come home wagging their tails behind them." She no doubt is still waiting for them to come home. Lambs do not come home on their own. They are lost unless someone intervenes for them.

In the same way, inanimate objects are lost without some kind of intervention. I lose things all the time. I'm a loser—especially when it comes to car keys. When I lose my car keys, I know I can't whistle for them and expect them to drop into my pocket. Christ is making an important point in the way He structures these stories; He is showing that those who are lost are hopelessly and helplessly lost unless He steps in.

Even the prodigal son would have remained utterly lost if his father hadn't forgiven him. Many people think the great offense of this story is that the boy spent all his money in riotous living. But that's not the point of the story at all. The point is the son's tremendous offense against his father.

First, he asked for his inheritance ahead of time. In the Palestinian culture, even today, if a child does such a thing, it's as though he were saying to his father, "I wish you were dead."

Second, in addition to insulting his father, he cashed out his assets and left for a foreign land. He took his portion of the estate, his dad's personal social security, and he wasted it all on selfish living. He brought shame to his family. Then he ended up working on a Gentile pig farm. What was a nice Jewish boy doing in a place like that? If we properly understand the Eastern mind-set when this story was told, we know that the Pharisees held no hope for that boy. They would never countenance a father's forgiving a son who had behaved the way this prodigal son did. Such a boy would have no hope unless his father intervened and forgave him.

This does away with all the nonsense we hear to the effect that we're not really dead in sin, just "wounded." All we have to do is get up, pull ourselves up by the bootstraps, think positively, and get going. But God's Word makes abundantly clear that we are dead in our trespasses and sins. Unless there is some intervention from God, we are hopelessly and helplessly lost.

God cares because He has suffered a loss, and He has proved that He cares by choosing to intervene on behalf of those who are helplessly lost. That is why Jesus Christ was at the center of that crowd. That is why Jesus Christ hung on the cross and shed His blood. That is why the Father touched Christ's tomb and brought Him to life, proving that He can give life to all who come to Him, cling to the cross, and receive the Savior for themselves.

These stories tell us that *all* the lost have worth to God—every one of them. We've already talked about what a sheep means to a shepherd, what a coin means to a widow, what a son means to a father. Look around you. Look at the businessman who keeps cheating you with contracts that are dishonest while you're trying to live with integrity. God cares for him. Look at the person who keeps offending you, even though you're extending love and concern. God cares for her. Every sinner in this world has value to God. When Christ told these stories, He depicted things of inherently high value to the persons who had lost them: a sheep, a coin, a son. Today we can apply that principle to people in our culture who seem beyond salvation: the doctor who performs abortions, the leaders of the gay and lesbian movement, godless legislators, the crack pusher, the prostitute, and the AIDS victim who could care less how he got the disease. God sees all of these lost ones as having worth.

TRANSFERABLE TRUTH

Christ told these three stories not only to prove that if God were here, He'd be right at the core of the crowd with the lost; He told them to instruct those who say, "Who cares about the lost?" "Who cares about the tax collectors and sinners of our day?" We say we love God and we say we belong to Him, but are we willing to live by His agenda? Isn't it fair to assume that if God has a heart for the lost, those who belong to Him should have the same agenda?

God wants us to hate the darkness and fight its influence. But He also wants us to remember that in the darkness are people precious to God—people we, too, should love.

Within these stories, then, we find profound truths concerning ways we might reorder our values in relation to the lost. Christ Himself speaks to our hearts, thoughts, and actions concerning all those for whom He died.

Repenting of Prejudice

The first practical lesson we can learn from these stories is that if we are to adopt God's agenda for the lost, we must repent of our prejudices. "Wait a minute," you say. "I'm not prejudiced. I got over that in the sixties!"

We're not prejudiced—or are we? Imagine yourself walking through a mall, and suddenly a group of teenagers approaches. They're wearing T-shirts bearing grotesque images. Their heads are shaved on one side, with green, yellow, purple, and red spikes coming out the other side. Their earrings dangle, and their leather wristbands have metal spikes on them. As they come toward you, what are you going to say? "Hi, gang, how are you doing today? Hope you have a wonderful time in the mall"? Or do you, as you walk by them as far away as possible, think, *Lord they have terrible needs. Thank you that I'm not like that?*

"Maybe we *are* prejudiced," you might argue, "but I've read this chapter of the Bible, and I don't see anything in it about prejudice." Actually, why are the Pharisees standing at the fringe of the crowd saying, "He spends time with people like that"? Because they have a problem with prejudice. And just as their prejudices built barriers among the people Christ cared for, so prejudices build barriers between us and those God loves through us. As soon as we start mentally segregating different kinds of people, saying, "They don't have worth," we stop feeling the need to communicate Christ to them. Prejudice is a serious problem.

That is why Jesus Christ said God the Father is like a shepherd. In a Pharisee's mind, a shepherd was at the low end of the caste system—with the tanners, tax collectors, and prostitutes. Did you ever wonder why David didn't get invited when the prophet Samuel came to his family's house? Somebody had to watch the sheep, and since he was the youngest child in the family, the role of shepherd had been relegated to him—all the way at the bottom of the family ladder. Pharisees had a deep prejudice against shepherds. They were probably shocked to hear Christ indicate in the first story that "God is like a *shepherd* who has lost a sheep."

Similarly, the Pharisees had a low opinion of women. They viewed women as chattel, sources of defilement, sources of temptation, and the guilty parties in cases of adultery. If a Pharisee was walking down a sidewalk and saw a woman walking toward him, he would cross the street and walk down the other side. But Christ said, "God is like a *woman* who lost a coin."

We have already discussed what a phenomenal offense the wayward son committed against his father. The Pharisees would have said that the father should never forgive that boy. So Jesus said, "God is like the *forgiving father* of a prodigal son."

In all three stories Christ uses a spirit of conviction to back our prejudices against the wall. We have to remember that in order to care for the lost, we first need to address the problem of prejudice that builds barriers between us and certain kinds of people.

I grew up during the "hippie" era, and since I had all the biblical values imbued into me by home and church, I really didn't have time for hippies. Because I had worked during high school and had saved up my money, by my second year of college I had enough money to buy a Volkswagen® bug. I remember one time in college, as I was driving up an interstate on-ramp, I saw a hippie hitchhiking. He had long hair, tattered clothes, thick beard, a knapsack, and a guitar. I blew past him, thinking in my self-righteousness, *If you want a ride, why don't you get a job and buy your own car?*

About a quarter of a mile down the interstate, God started working me over. It was as though He said, "Stowell, could we talk about that hippie?"

"Sure."

He said, "I just heard what you said about him. Did you ever think of looking at him the way I look at him?"

"I just did, Lord. You don't like him either. I know You don't like him. Look at what he stands for: free sex, drugs, anti-authority, anti-establishment. Lord, he is against everything You're for. I know You don't like people like that."

It was as though the Lord said, "Wrong. I died for him. If he were the only person alive, I still would have died on the cross for him." Suddenly, I realized that I had a real problem with prejudice.

One of the most wonderful things about many of God's people today is a genuine concern about missions—the desire to reach the world for Christ. We're all into missions, it seems. But guess what's happening? In America today, the world is moving to our cities and to our neighborhoods. The mission fields are coming from all over the world to us. That sounds exciting . . . unless you live in a nice suburb, and suddenly your neighbor puts up a "For Sale" sign, sells the house, and four weeks later a big truck pulls up. As you look through the blinds, you notice that the people moving in aren't like you. They don't have the same ethnic background. They don't have the same color of skin. They may not even speak English very well.

What happens then to your zeal for missions? Do you say, "Fantastic! God has brought the mission field to my neighborhood! Now I can be a missionary"? Do you yell to your spouse, "Sweetheart, let's fall to our knees and start praying. We've been wanting to be missionaries all our lives, and now we get to do it"? It's doubtful. More likely, we turn to our spouse and say, "Well, sweetheart, do you know a good realtor?"

When I was a little kid in church, we used to sing a song that went like this: "Red and yellow, black and white, all are precious in His sight." Why did we stop singing that? Did we get too sophisticated? Or did that song get a little too convicting? We will go nowhere with the gospel until we look at every single person in our world as having worth to God. If we're going to think correctly about the lost, we need to repent of our prejudices.

SERIOUS SEEKING

Once we've repented of our prejudices, it is time to commit ourselves to being seekers of the lost. Let's look again at Christ's first story in Luke 15. The principles are rich. In fact, we can find four definite traits of a serious seeker of the lost.

In verse 4 Christ asks, "What man among you, if he has a hundred sheep and has lost one of them, does not . . . leave . . ?" First and foremost, seekers are leavers. We need to learn to break out of our holy huddles in order to seek the lost.

If we are ever going to be effective for the gospel, we've got to leave our comfort zones, get out there with the lost, and rub shoulders with them in order to win them for Christ. Seekers are leavers.

Second, notice that the seriously seeking shepherd leaves the ninety-nine in open pasture and goes after the single lost sheep until he finds it. Seekers are finders. Unfortunately, some of us go out for only brief little forays into the world of the lost. "I went out there," we say. "I saw five of them. They're really out there—no kidding! But I'm sure glad to be back! Whew, what an experience."

Jesus asked, "Doesn't one who cares for the lost—the shepherd of the sheep—leave the comfort zone and stay out there until he finds it?" The answer is yes! Seekers are finders.

Third, in verse 5 we read that "when he has found it, he lays it on his shoulders." Seekers are bearers. At this point some of us are thinking, *Whoa, time out! Do you mean to say that if I happen to lead a business associate to Christ, or a neighbor, or even a stranger, I need to bear him or her back to the safety of the fold?* That's right. *You mean I've got to invite him to that monthly potluck we've been going to for nineteen years with the same four couples? Ask him to sit with me in church? Follow up and help him make the transition from the habits of darkness to the principles and thoughts of the kingdom?* Absolutely correct. Serious seekers are not only leavers and finders; they are bearers who take the precious lamb that's been found, put it on their shoulders, and bear it safely back to the fold.

Finally, if you are committed to being a serious seeker, you will not only be a leaver, a finder, and a bearer—you will also be a rejoicer. The shepherd returned rejoicing. In fact, Luke's particular literary approach underscores one grand theme—rejoicing. Why did Luke emphasize the theme of rejoicing? Because the scribes and Pharisees were murmuring and grumbling! Christ was saying emphatically that their prejudicial grumbling reflected the fact that they didn't have the heart of heaven.

UNBRIDLED JOY

As I minister in churches across America, I have become concerned about some of our churches. It seems that many of our churches have been laid out, nailed shut, and buried six feet under. What has happened to our joy? What has happened to our spirit of celebration? We are on the victor's side. We've been redeemed. But we have no joy. Where did it go?

There could be many reasons, but one thing is sure—there is a good chance that in a church without joy means that the lost haven't been sought for a long, long time. Conversely, if we begin to see a revival of caring for the lost and spending of time at the core of the crowd, we are going to be surprised at the joy that suddenly is infused into our congregations. Why? Because seekers are rejoicers.

Some time ago, when we were in the process of moving to Moody Bible Institute, we had four Sundays free. So we decided to visit several different churches on those open weekends. We went to a leading black Baptist church, and we sat through their service for a full two and a half hours. It was wonderful! The choir was terrific. The preacher preached a great message. And at the close of that message, he gave an invitation to take a public stand for Christ. The choir began to sing, and the congregation began to join the choir. They sang—but no one came forward. Then, after what I thought was quite an extended period of time, one man stood up in the back and started walking slowly down the aisle. Do you know what that congregation did? They broke out in spontaneous applause. I loved it! And I thought, *How much like heaven this is—when even one comes, all heaven rejoices.*

Where do we stand? With Christ at the core of the crowd? Or at the fringe with the Pharisees, a little yellow sign around our neck saying, "Who Cares?" If God cares, we too must care. He has sent us, just as He sent Christ. Therefore, we too must repent of our prejudice so that there are no barriers, and commit ourselves to being serious seekers—leavers, finders, bearers, and rejoicers.

Before we moved to Chicago, we used to take our children to the museums in Chicago at Christmastime. And while we were in the city, we would do a little Christmas shopping, too.

I will never forget the time when, in a huge multi-tiered mall, we suddenly looked around and discovered that our little boy Matthew was gone. He was probably about four years old at the time, and instantly, all the horror stories about little children being kidnapped in malls filled our hearts. Immediately, our assignment changed. No longer was it leisurely shopping. It was time to find the lost! That boy had phenomenal value to us, so we took up our assignment with zeal and urgency. I went out into the parking lot yelling, "Matthew! Matthew!" I felt like a total fool, but the cause was far more important than how I felt. I didn't find him. When I came back inside, Martie hadn't found him, either. Nor had my mother. But then we saw my dad walking down the aisle with little Matthew in hand—blond hair, glasses, smiling, and totally untraumatized. My dad had found him at the candy counter, standing there with his little hands behind his back, just looking at all the candy.

The interesting thing is that Matthew didn't look lost; but he was. He didn't know the phenomenal danger he was in; but it was real.

You and I move about in a world where the people around us don't look lost and have no understanding of the eternal danger they are in. But their lostness is real, and the danger is acute.

We must ask ourselves, *Who cares for these people? Who is going to seek them? Who is going to keep looking for them until they are found?*

As we brighten the darkness with a heart of compassion, we proclaim through attitude and action that in Him is life, and this life is the *light* of men (cf. John 1:4).

POSTSCRIPT

A Quiet Revolution

The fabled Rip Van Winkle slept for twenty years, and when he awoke his world had dramatically changed. So had he. If we are not careful, Christians in America may become the Rip Van Winkles of our era. Our world has changed, and this changing world threatens to change us. Surprisingly, those of us who are to be in the world but not of the world now seem to be very much of this world.

In essence, this absorption into the culture has influenced the way we think about basic issues of life, such as pain, happiness, success, prosperity, purpose, rights, privileges, and people. It is time to change our minds. We must to embrace the biblical strategy that calls us to become light in the darkness. The strategy is not a quick fix. It will require a willingness to alter our thinking and subsequently our lives. It will require courageous persistence.

As the culture becomes increasingly hostile, the territory of our minds, homes, and churches will become an increasingly sacred area for us to guard jealously against the intrusion of the darkness. Throughout history it has been heart, mind, home, and church that have been impregnable fortresses when courageously protected. They have provided safe havens where the light is cultivated, nurtured, and encouraged. Yet these safety zones must be more than fortresses. They must become launching pads from which a strategic offensive is staged—the offensive of the personal proclamation of rightness from every aspect of our existence. Then, as the decay and despair of the darkness deepens, the unquenchable light will prevail.

The psalmist asks, "If the foundations are destroyed what can the righteous do?" He answers his own question as the psalm unfolds.

In the Lord I take refuge;
How can you say to my soul, "Flee as a bird to your mountain;
For, behold, the wicked bend the bow,
They make ready their arrow upon the string,
To shoot in darkness at the upright in heart.
If the foundations are destroyed,
What can the righteous do?"
The Lord is in His holy temple, the Lord's throne is in heaven;
His eyes behold, His eyelids test the sons of men.
The Lord tests the righteous and the wicked,
And the one who loves violence His soul hates.
Upon the wicked He will rain snares;
Fire and brimstone and burning wind will be the portion of their cup.
For the Lord is righteous; He loves righteousness;
The upright will behold His face.

(Psalm 11)

The question before us now is, Will the church dare to challenge the deepening darkness with the light of unshakable righteousness coming from the lives of her people?